VARGHESE M.THOMAS

THE FINAL Reckoning

BlueRoseONE.com
Stories Matter
NewDelhi • London

BLUEROSE PUBLISHERS
India | U.K.

BlueRose ONE
Stories Matter
NewDelhi • London

For permissions requests or inquiries regarding this publication, please contact:

BLUEROSE PUBLISHERS
www.BlueRoseONE.com
info@bluerosepublishers.com
+91 8882 898 898
+4407342408967

ISBN: 978-93-7139-590-8

Cover design: Daksh
Typesetting: Tanya Raj Upadhyay

First Edition: December 2025

Acknowledgment

I am profoundly grateful to God for guiding my journey and granting me the wisdom, strength, and perseverance to bring this book to life.

My heartfelt thanks to my wonderful wife for her constant encouragement and honest feedback, which helped shape my thoughts and writing. To my two amazing children, Vanessa and Shawn - you inspire me every day to strive harder and aim higher.

I lovingly remember my father, whose wisdom and values continue to guide me, and my mother, whose boundless love and support have always been my strength.

I am genuinely thankful to my family, friends, and former colleagues for their faith in me and their constant encouragement, which kept me motivated throughout this journey. Finally, I would like to extend my sincere appreciation to the dedicated team at Blue Rose Publishing for their commitment and hard work in bringing this book to life.

About Varghese M Thomas

Varghese M. Thomas is a globally recognised communications leader, known for shaping narratives that inspire trust, enhance reputations, and create lasting impact. With almost thirty years of experience advising C-suite executives and guiding influential brands, he is an award-winning strategist celebrated for bringing clarity and insight to complex challenges. His career includes leadership roles at multinational corporations such as Intel, Cisco, and BlackBerry, as well as leading Indian conglomerates like TVS Motor, Greaves Cotton, and Tata Electronics—providing him with broad expertise across both international and domestic markets. A respected thought leader, he has contributed to leading publications and books on communications, and most recently, made his fiction debut with Whispers in the Shadows.

THE FINAL RECKONING

Table of Contents

Chapter 1: The Streets of Goa

The air in Panaji bears rich narratives. Heavily imbued with the fragrances of salt and spices, it navigates through the labyrinthine streets, whispering tales through the swaying coconut palms and the distant murmurs of the Arabian Sea. The aroma of freshly ground masalas mingles with the briny breeze, an intoxicating blend that seeps into the senses and clings to skin and clothing long after the day is done.

The bustling roads, alive with the chatter of vendors selling their goods and the constant honking of mopeds, maintain a rhythm of their own—a heartbeat that pulses beneath the city's ever-moving facade. Market stalls overflow with juicy mangoes, bundles of cinnamon sticks, and strings of dried red chillies that shimmer like embers under the midday sun.

Fishermen, with sun-kissed faces and marks from the sea, happily gather their day's catch. Their lively voices blend with the bustling sounds as they cheerfully haggle with women gracefully balancing baskets on their hips. The docks feel like a magical place, where colourful boats in shades of blue and red gently sway with the tide, sharing stories of generations who have thrived and faced the ocean's challenges bravely.

The very walls of Panaji are steeped in history, whispering tales of a bygone era. The historic Latin Quarter, known as Fontainhas, stands as a testament to the Portuguese who ruled Goa for over four centuries, with their influence still visible in the pastel-coloured houses featuring ornate balconies and tiled rooftops. Cobblestone streets wind past hidden chapels, their whitewashed façades shining under the tropical sun, where prayers are said in both Konkani and Portuguese. The aroma of freshly baked pão drifts from bakeries that still use wood-fired ovens, a tradition passed down through generations of Goan Catholics who uphold their way of life despite the encroachment of modernity.

Life in this region is more than just surviving; it involves celebrating daily rituals and rhythms. The fishermen start their day before dawn, casting nets into the unpredictable sea, hopeful for a good catch that will shape their day's fortunes. Market women, dressed beautifully in vibrant sarees, carefully arrange their produce in organised patterns. You can hear the cheerful sounds of bangles clinking as they exchange coins and share warm conversations in a charming blend of Konkani and Hindi.

Shopkeepers position themselves behind wooden counters, observing the world with the patience typical of those who have seen it all before. In the evenings, as the sun dips below the horizon, families gather outside their homes, sharing tales over steaming cups of chai or glasses of feni, the local cashew liquor that, although harsh on the throat, warms the soul.

Children happily scamper barefoot along the winding streets of old Goa, their joyful laughter like cheerful birdsong filling the lively air. They playfully dart through the crowds, curious tourists with cameras hanging from their necks, warm-hearted locals dressed in simple cotton clothes, and friendly shopkeepers proudly displaying their wares under vibrant, colourful awnings. The ground beneath their tiny feet is a charming mix of dust, cobblestone, and uneven tarmac, whispering tales of the passing time in this magical place. Their voices rise and fall like ocean tides, blending with the cheerful clang of bicycle bells, the sputtering hum of scooters weaving through the crowd, and the soft murmurs of an older woman selling marigold garlands by the church steps. Her wrinkled hands, moving with practised ease, string the flowers as their sweet fragrance mingles with the warm, salty breeze gently drifting in from the Arabian Sea.

Not far from where the children play, church bells toll in the distance, their echoes drifting through the air, marking the passage of time with a measured rhythm. The bells belong to an ancient ecclesiastical building characterised by high, whitewashed walls and a towering steeple, a remnant of the Portuguese who once inhabited this place. Inside, candles flicker before saints with solemn faces, their expressions preserved in time; meanwhile, prayers fill the vast space, rising towards the ornate ceiling in a nearly musical cadence.

Across the square, in a dimly lit tavern, the mournful sounds of a fado singer drift through the night, her voice rich with longing and heartbreak. Sitting in the corner with a Portuguese guitar resting against his knee, an elderly musician plucks each note with a precision that reflects years spent perfecting the craft. The air is thick with the aroma of spiced curries and the deep, earthy scent of port wine poured generously into glasses that catch the glow of lantern light. A few patrons sway gently in their seats, lost in the bittersweet melancholy of the music, their eyes reflecting distant memories.

In Goa, the past and present coexist not as distant relatives but as intertwined entities, inseparable in their embrace. Colonial-era buildings, characterised by their weathered yet dignified façades, stand close to neon-lit establishments pulsating with contemporary rhythms.

The ancient banyan trees, with their thick, gnarled roots, extend their welcoming branches over narrow alleyways, providing cool shade to cheerful street vendors selling a delightful array of items, including feni and beautifully woven scarves. Serenity and vibrancy intertwine in a gentle dance as the joyful sound of wind chimes harmonises seamlessly with the lively beats of drums from a bustling late-night beach party.

The fragrant aroma of seafood infused with coconut and wood-fired bread fills the modest kitchens, where grandmothers carefully stir bubbling pots with wooden ladles polished over generations. Street-side stalls display pyramids of ripe mangoes, their golden skins gleaming beneath the warm glow of hanging bulbs. Vendors loudly announce their offerings in a mix of Konkani, Portuguese, and English, their voices capturing the harmonious spirit of a region that has experienced centuries of change while remaining true to its identity.

By the riverside, fishermen gather their nets, the silver shapes of freshly caught fish shimmering under the moonlight. The wooden boats gently rock against the docks, their hulls painted in vibrant shades of blue and red, labelled with names like "Santa Maria" and "Blessing of the Sea." A few metres away, a group of young men cluster around a makeshift table, immersed in a lively game of cards, their laughter and exclamations punctuating the night-time atmosphere.

Further along the shoreline, where the sand meets the turbulent waves, bonfires cast a warm glow in the darkness, their flames reaching skyward. Tourists from distant lands sit cross-legged, sharing stories and bottles of local spirits, their conversations weaving a rich tapestry of accents and languages. The roar of the ocean echoes in the background, its timeless melody blending with the distant strains of a violin played by a lone musician perched on a rock, his silhouette against the horizon.

The night unfolds in layers, each revealing a different facet of Goa's essence. Here, history speaks through crumbling forts, where faith finds its voice in candlelit chapels and incense-filled temples, and where joy dances in the streets, unburdened by time. The children, still playing in the dust, will grow up knowing this land as both heritage and home, a place where yesterday and tomorrow meet in a warm embrace as inviting as the Goan sun.

Among them was Leo Carlos, a slender young boy with dark eyes that seemed to notice more than others might see. His feet were bare, and his clothes were patched and worn; yet there was a defiance in how he moved through the streets. He was swift—faster than the shopkeepers chasing him after he steals a mango from their carts, and quicker than the older boys trying to trap him in an alley. He knew every shortcut and hidden passageway that run through the city like veins beneath its surface.

His father, Manuel Carlos, was a fisherman with calloused hands and a history of broken promises, often absent. He had a fiery temperament that could flare up suddenly, like a sudden storm. Despite dreaming big, the sea often took away those dreams along with his earnings. His absences could last weeks or even months, leaving behind promises of better days that seemed just out of reach. When he was home, he often turned to alcohol, and the house thickened with unspoken resentment, fear, and a quiet grief no one dared to name.

The house was modest—a dilapidated one-bedroom structure with peeling lime-washed walls and a low tin roof that groaned with every passing gust. The floor was uneven, with patches of mismatched tiles and cement. A second, smaller room had been crudely fashioned for Liza and Leo—more an afterthought than a proper space—its partition made from an old bedsheet, plywood, and rusted nails. It offered little privacy and less comfort.

Elena, Leo's mother, quietly embraced her role of keeping their family close and connected. Her gentle resilience shone through her dark, expressive eyes, hinting at wonderful stories she cherished deep in her heart. Each morning, long before the sun's first light, she rose with quiet determination, her hands carefully preparing delicate sweets and warm, fragrant bread to sell at the bustling market. She was the steady anchor at the centre of their family life, an unbreakable thread that held them all together. This invisible glue made everything feel safe and secure, even when life's challenges tried to pull them apart.

Elena was the only daughter of Don Rafael, the town's most revered schoolteacher. A man celebrated for his wisdom, firm discipline, and deep affection for literature and learning. Their home, set on a gentle slope overlooking the bay, was a sanctuary of peace and richness, filled with the rustling of turning pages, the soft cadence of her father's voice delivering lessons, and the constant aroma of her mother's blooming roses and freshly baked bread.

While her father taught her the importance of thought and observation, it was her mother who introduced her to the quiet joy of creating. A talented baker, Elena's mother would rise early each day, her hands coated in flour, humming softly as she kneaded, shaped, and transformed the simplest ingredients into warmth and delight. Even as a child, Elena was captivated by the magic. She would spend hours beside her mother, observing, her small hands imitating the motions–learning to fold, to stir, and to wait.

Over time, the kitchen became her second classroom, a place where patience and instinct reigned. She grew to love the tactile rhythm of baking and how it brought comfort to others. From her mother, she didn't only inherit recipes, she inherited heart.

Manuel, on the other hand, was the son of a fisherman and a seamstress. He lived in the cramped quarters of the old town, where the scent of salt and fish clung to every surface, and the sea's moods dictated the rhythm of daily life. Manuel's hands were already rough from helping his father mend nets, and his clothes, though always clean, showed unmistakable signs of wear. He attended the same school where Don Rafael taught, yet he was more often found gazing out of the window at the restless sea rather than paying attention to the lessons indoors.

Their worlds were divided not just by distance but also by class, expectations, and the unseen boundaries drawn by tradition. Yet, fate, with its peculiar sense of irony, united them. It all started with a book.

One afternoon, Elena stayed after class, her head bent over a poetry book borrowed from her father's library. The classroom was nearly empty when Manuel, tasked with cleaning the blackboards as a punishment for another daydream, lingered at the back. He watched her, captivated by how her lips moved silently and how her fingers traced the lines of verse.

Gathering his courage, Manuel stepped forward. "What are you reading?" he asked, his voice tentative.

Elena looked up, startled, then smiled. "It's Neruda. Do you like poetry?"

He shrugged, feeling embarrassed. "I've never really read any."

She held out the book, her eyes inviting. "Would you like me to read to you?"

That marked the start of something special. Every afternoon, they eagerly found small reasons to linger a little longer after school—perhaps tidying their desks more slowly, gladly volunteering to run minor errands for the teachers, or choosing to take the longer, winding route around the playground. Elena loved reading aloud beneath the lush tamarind trees, her voice gentle yet confident, sharing stories from distant lands. Manuel always sat beside her, sometimes with his eyes closed, dreaming of the worlds she conjured. Occasionally, she would ask him about the sea, its moods, its rhythms and he would proudly recount stories of storms that devoured ships, dolphins racing by at dusk, nets full or empty, and the horizon glowing like molten silver at dawn.

During those peaceful moments, they discovered a shared desire for freedom, for beauty, and for something beyond the tired streets of their small town and the expectations awaiting them at home. Their friendship, gentle yet fiercely guarded, blossomed in secret hours under the old mango tree behind the school. Elena would bring him old, cherished books with notes in the margins; Manuel would gift her seashells, pieces of driftwood, and stories his father shared. They laughed often, sometimes arguing about poetry, politics, or the meaning of courage, only to find themselves growing even closer.

One beautiful evening, as the sky turned into a stunning canvas of orange and gold, and the sweet smell of ripe mangoes filled the air, Manuel gently took Elena's hand. "I wish I could give you more," he whispered, his voice full of longing, carrying the heavy, unspoken feelings of his heart.

She gently squeezed his hand, her eyes shining with warmth and certainty. "You already have," she whispered. "You've shared stories that broadened my world, brought laughter when I needed it most, and created a place where I can truly be myself. That's more than I ever expected to have."

Their love resembled a delicate, treasured secret garden, carefully nurtured and valued. But secrets tend to surface eventually. Rumours began to circulate. Elena, the schoolteacher's sweet daughter, was seen strolling with the fisherman's boy. Her father was deeply distressed and firmly told her she could no longer see Manuel, urging her to concentrate on her studies and her ambitions. Manuel was also cautioned to keep away, risking the possibility of expulsion.

But love, once kindled, often endures and radiates warmly for a long time.

Over the following years, they tenderly kept their secret ritual alive, subtly slipping handwritten letters into the hollow of the old mango tree. In bustling markets, their eyes would meet amid the lively crowd, with their fingers gently grazing as they passed each other. Those stolen moments became truly precious to them. Every challenge they encountered only strengthened their bond and imbued them with a quiet, unwavering determination.

Finally, Elena reached her breaking point. She faced her father with courage, her voice calm but her heartbeat racing. "I love him," she said bravely. "I understand what I might be losing, but I can't keep living a lie."

Don Rafael saw the determination shining in his daughter's eyes and gently relented, although there was a hint of sadness in his heart. He decided to meet Manuel to get to know him better. The encounter was a bit tense; however, Manuel, feeling nervous but earnest, shared his dreams, his deep respect for Elena, and his sincere desire to build a brighter future. Over time, Don Rafael's initial anger eased, creating space for a cautious, reluctant acceptance and a flicker of hope.

Their humble wedding was a charming and intimate celebration at a small church with a stunning sea view. Elena looked lovely in her simple dress, her hair adorned with wildflowers, adding a touch of nature's beauty. Manuel stood tall and proud, with his eyes filled with love. Their families gathered–some joyful, others a bit emotional, but everyone felt the special bond that united them, celebrating this wonderful union.

The early years of their marriage brimmed with hope and promise. Manuel committed himself to long hours on the boats, eager to secure a bright future for his new family. Elena, though inexperienced with hardship, displayed remarkable resilience and adaptability. She often rose before dawn to walk to the shore, lantern in hand, watching the horizon until his boat appeared against the breaking waves. During the monsoons, she would wait in the pouring rain, her shawl soaked through, refusing to leave until she saw him step safely onto the sand. When money was tight, she would laugh away her hunger and insist on saving the last piece of bread for him, brushing his cheek with flour-dusted hands as if it were a feast.

Elena quickly learnt to mend nets, stretch their meals, and find joy in the simple rhythms of their life together. There were evenings when they danced barefoot in the rain, nights when they whispered kisses beneath a starry sky, and quiet hours when they dreamt of a future where their children would always feel safe, loved, and cared for. In those moments, their love seemed strong enough to carry them through anything.

Over the years, reality began to weigh heavily. The sea, once full of wonder, now felt like a difficult challenge. Manuel's income was small and often lost to storms or misfortune. Elena, as a mother, did her best by taking on extra work, baking bread, sewing clothes, and doing everything she could to keep her family afloat. The children grew up quickly, their needs increasing, and their hunger always present, like a steady ache that would not go away.

Leo often admired her as she diligently kneaded the dough, her fingers moving with a gentle rhythm, almost as if she was trying to sprinkle hope into the very fabric of their everyday lives. She never complained aloud, but Leo could sense the weariness in her sighs at the end of each day, feeling the heavy burden of their struggle. Years of hardship had hardened her, replacing softer qualities with a calm, strong resolve that guided every action and sacrifice she made.

Liza Carlos was a shining beacon in her family's modest home, her laughter a sound that could lift even the darkest days. Being four years younger than her brother Leo, Liza was known for her boundless curiosity and sharp, quick mind. She inherited her mother's expressive, dark eyes - eyes that seemed to hold a thousand untold stories and had an uncanny ability to sense when silence meant more than words.

From her earliest days, Liza's world was marked by scarcity. Hunger was a constant companion, and the soles of her feet grew tough from running barefoot over the hard-packed earth and uneven stones surrounding their home. Yet, these hardships did little to dampen her spirit. If anything, they instilled in her a resilience that shone through in the way she carried herself, her head held high and her eyes bright with possibility.

Leo, her older brother, was both her protector and partner in mischief. He was often full of enthusiasm, always eager to help with chores or to shield Liza from their father's stern words. Leo's strong sense of responsibility developed early, influenced by their father's absence and their mother's quiet resilience. Despite these responsibilities, Leo never let them diminish his love for Liza. He cared for her with a watchfulness that stemmed from deep love.

Their days often started before the sun rose. Their mother, Elena, was already busy in the tiny kitchen, sleeves rolled up and hair tied back, kneading dough with fierce determination, as if fighting poverty itself. The rhythmic thump of her hands on the wooden board echoed through the house like a gentle lullaby in reverse–a steady, comforting beat that reminded Liza that even in chaos, the world kept turning. Most mornings, Liza would softly tiptoe into the kitchen, rub the sleep from her eyes, and quietly steal a small piece of dough or a tiny bit of jaggery. Elena would playfully wave a flour-dusted spoon, her tone filled with mock outrage. "Thieves don't get breakfast!" she'd say with a smile, laughing as she let her daughter sneak another bite.

Once Elena finished her morning chores and headed to the market, arms laden with warm bread and sticky sweet buns, looking every bit like a queen on a grocery adventure, the world outside their cosy little house burst with life. The narrow, dusty alleys felt like secret passageways to hidden kingdoms. Sunlight streamed through the neem trees like a spotlight from a magic show, and the open fields shimmered with hope and possibility.

Liza, with her lively imagination, could turn anything into magic. Stones became treasures, sticks turned into swords, and the old mango tree out back often became a pirate ship one day and a royal castle the next. Leo, always eager to join in, followed her with a big, happy grin, ready to be the knight, the lookout, or the dragon depending on their adventure. Liza, the fearless leader of their imaginative missions, declared herself ruler of entire empires before breakfast. "Today, I am Queen Liza the Bold," she'd announce, holding a broomstick like a royal sceptre. "And Sir Liza the Brave Knight."

Leo, always so grounded yet full of life, would sigh contentedly and pull out his carefully drawn map, crafted on the back of an old homework sheet, no less. "You can't be both. That's against the rules of the Kingdom of

Reason," he'd say, his eyes sparkling with fun. Together, they would explore jungles, uncover hidden pirate treasures, and defend imaginary castles–always returning home just before sunset, tired, dusty, and smiling from ear to ear.

One of their favourite games was "Market Day," where Liza enjoyed pretending to be a wealthy señora while Leo played the role of a clever merchant. They used pebbles for coins and leaves for wares, happily negotiating, joking, and laughing until their stomachs ached. These joyful moments were more than just fun; they were small acts of hope and gentle rebellions against the boundaries of their world.

Although they were very close, the siblings had their fair share of differences. Liza was brave and outspoken, always ready to ask questions and stand up for her beliefs. A few years ago, she bravely confronted a group of older boys who tried to bully Leo, holding her ground with a fierceness that even surprised her brother. "You don't scare me," she said confidently, her voice calm and steady. The boys eventually backed off, and Leo looked at her with a mixture of pride and a little frustration.

Liza was a lively burst of energy and sunshine; a girl who grew up with scraped knees, big dreams, and a burning fire in her heart. Brave and determined, she was never afraid to speak her mind or stand up for what she believed in, even if it meant getting into trouble. But deep down, that fiery spirit was matched by a loving heart, protective of her family, kind to strangers, and always quick with a joke to brighten heavy moods. She laughed loudly, ran barefoot through fields carefree, and truly believed she could shape the world, not just inherit it. Nothing ever really frightened Liza.

Leo, for his part, was always quite considerate, carefully planning ahead. He genuinely cared about what the future might hold, worrying about their mother's health and the next meal they'd share. Sometimes, his concerns spilt over in frustration, and he'd snap at Liza for her carefree ways. But those moments didn't last long. Liza had an exceptional talent for lifting his spirits—whether through a funny joke, a catchy song, or simply sitting quietly beside him, her calming presence always brought him comfort.

Leo noticed things others brushed past. He saw how his mother's hands lingered a second longer on the empty rice tin before she smiled, or how his father's shoulders sagged when he thought no one was watching. In those moments, Leo felt a quiet bond with their struggles, as if carrying a piece of the weight himself. At times, he would find his mother sitting silently at the table, gathering her strength in the stillness. He knew she loved him and Liza deeply, yet no matter how boundless that love was, it could never quite ease the gnawing of their hungry stomachs.

But on the streets, survival came first, slipping guavas into his bag as if it were second nature. His sharp eyes studied the bakers, who turned away at a stolen roll and who might chase him with laughter and mock scolding. When fights came, he held his composure; bruised fists and split knuckles were just part of the game. In Panaji's crowded alleys, weakness was never an option.

There were other boys like him, shadows of the streets who had already sacrificed their innocence to hunger and hardship. Rafiq, the clever son of a cobbler, showed Leo how to slip through the narrowest gaps in the crowded market. Deepu, a boy with a mischievous grin and a talent for distraction, gently guided him on how to make a quick getaway. They were his friends in surviving each day, bonded not by family but by the need to get by. Together, they faced the world in a quiet contest, where losing meant going to bed hungry.

Leo hungered for more than survival; he yearned a life with weight and meaning. In Panaji's crowded market, he slipped past vendors' reaching hands, hunger biting at him with a force deeper than the need for food. What he craved was power, the kind that made the world step aside at his presence. He desired respect so unshakable it would free him from ever having to steal again. While boys his age chased kites and marbles, Leo measured life in terms of endurance and strength. He wanted more than play. He wanted a life where struggle bent to his will, where dignity was not pleaded for but commanded–the kind of ambition that could forge a man, or break him.

When Lucas Dada first appeared, he carried an air of authority that made him quite legendary in Panaji. People spoke about him with a mix of caution and respect, especially in bars and hidden market corners. His presence was so commanding that it would hush the crowd, encouraging men to speak softly and women to look away. He wasn't just a street hustler; he had cleverly shaped the city to work in his favour, demonstrating his shrewdness and influence.

Leo watched him closely, noting his attitude and the reactions of those nearby. Lucas had begun just like them, from the streets, but driven by fear. Leo aimed to reach that same level. He aspired to become someone who would always be remembered in the city, leaving a lasting legacy.

Leo told himself he could pay whatever price ambition demanded, certain that sacrifice was the only currency for the life he longed for, not yet aware of how steep that price might be.

Chapter 2
The House Behind the Spice Market

Leo's house was situated behind the bustling spice market, where every sound and scent seemed woven into his days. The shouts of vendors, the pungent air, and the laughter amid haggled bargains taught him early to observe and to read people as easily as reading books. At night, the beams above his bed groaned like ancient storytellers, while the paper-thin walls contained both dreams and worries. He carried with him his mother's comforting dawn prayers, the frequent storms of his parents' quarrels, and the quiet silences that, despite fatigue, wrapped them in calm strength.

The market truly felt like the heart of their world, alive with a vivid mix of colours, scents, and sounds. Vendors happily shared their prices, engaging in warm negotiations with customers amidst a cheerful blend of Konkani, Hindi, and Portuguese. Stalls were brimming with a wide variety of spices; saffron, cinnamon, and cardamom, each beautifully displayed in sparkling glass jars that reflected the sunlight like glittering treasures. The inviting aroma of fried samosas and steaming cups of chai filled the air, perfectly mingling with the sweet fragrance of jasmine garlands offered by the friendly floral merchants welcoming visitors at the entrance.

Leo treasured his childhood in this lively place, happily wandering through the narrow alleys and often glancing at the charming street performers who brought smiles to everyone by playing their flutes for a few rupees. He loved watching the wise elderly gentlemen relax at tea stalls, deeply engaged in lively talks about political issues. When he wasn't busy with school or helping his mother, he enjoyed taking peaceful walks to the docks, where he would watch fishermen return from the sea, their boats filled with the day's catch. He eagerly listened to their fascinating stories–tales of storms, mermaids, and exciting adventures with the ocean itself.

Despite their hardships, Leo found solace in life's simple pleasures.

He genuinely enjoyed hearing the joyful sound of his mother's laughter as she chatted with the other women at the market, such a rare moment of happiness that brought a warm glow to her usually tired face. He looked forward to the monsoons when the rain would softly tap against their tin roof, turning the dusty streets into flowing rivers. It was a special time for him to sit by the window and watch life slow down just a little. He also treasured the peaceful evenings when his father, sober but weary, would relax on their doorstep, sharing captivating stories about the stars and pointing out constellations, with his hands warmed by salt and fish.

Moments of peace were always fleeting. After Manuel returned from his fishing trips, an unspoken tension lingered heavily in the air. Would he have enough provisions to get through the month? Would he spend all his earnings at the pub before Elena could secretly save a little? Leo often saw the worry in his mother's eyes whenever his father arrived home late, carrying the scent of alcohol and murmuring about bad luck and broken dreams. Some evenings, voices would rise and dishes would be thrown, while on other nights, only silence reigned. More overwhelming than any storm.

As Leo grew older, he started to dream of escaping, not just from his home, but from the endless cycle of struggles that held his family back. He yearned for a brighter future, aiming for more than his father's life and the constant hard work his mother faced every day.

He dedicated himself entirely to his studies, eagerly absorbing every lesson from his teachers. Many nights, he sat silently under the soft glow of his tube light, lost in books and dreaming of a brighter future.

One evening, after a fierce storm kept the fishermen ashore, Manuel found a peaceful spot by the door, holding a bottle of cheap whisky. "The sea gives, and the sea takes," he whispered, his eyes fixed on the distant waves. "But it takes more than it gives." His voice was gentle and almost sacred, as if he were speaking with an ancient god. Next to him, Leo sat quietly, feeling the truth of those words echo deep in his heart.

He wondered why his father seemed to give up so easily and how failure affected him. Eventually, he decided to listen more carefully. That moment helped him realise that his father's anger wasn't just frustration; it was a result of tiredness. His father had been tirelessly battling tough times, worn out from hoping for change that never came, feeling sad as he watched his dreams fade away like grains of sand slipping through his fingers.

Elena called them in for dinner, her voice warm and sweet, filling the heavy air with a sense of comfort. They shared the meal in silence, the gentle candlelight flickering and casting playful shadows on the walls. Outside, the market gradually wound down, with the last cheerful vendors packing up their stalls, while the delightful scent of spices lingered like a treasured memory.

Leo realised that his life, much like the vibrant marketplace, would always be an exciting adventure full of movement, lively noise, and new challenges.

But deep down, he knew he wasn't like his father. He wouldn't let the sea take everything from him. He eagerly looked forward to a future beyond the house behind the spice market. When that moment arrived, he would cherish the wonderful aroma of cloves and turmeric, the warm memory of his mother's hands kneading dough with love, and the calming sound of his father's gentle voice sharing stories of the stars.

The Boy Who Ran

Leo initially learnt to navigate his environment before developing his language skills. The bustling streets of Panaji truly became his playground, classroom, and safe haven all in one. He wandered barefoot through winding alleyways, carefully avoiding carts and stray dogs as he explored secret corners that only street children dared to venture. He soon realised that the world was not very patient with those who hesitated or showed uncertainty.

Although he was small, he was exceptionally quick and agile! With a mischievous smile, he would quietly sneak mangoes from the vendor, who was often too busy counting to notice him. Time after time, he skilfully vanished into the crowd whenever trouble was near. He faced boys twice his size without fear, not just because of his strength, but because he had an incredible spirit that refused to give up. Those bruises he earned became his proud badges of honour, and every bit of pain was a valuable lesson that he warmly welcomed with open arms!

Even amid the hardships, there were precious moments to treasure. His mother's calming voice filled the air with loved lullabies as she gently braided his sister Liza's hair. The soothing taste of fresh, warm bread, still soft from the oven, was joyfully shared in the quiet alleys with other children who had so little to their names.

The ocean, so vast and endless, warmly beckoned him to sit for hours, completely mesmerised by the way the waves joyfully dance against the shore. He allowed his imagination to drift, dreaming of all the wonderful things that might be waiting for him just beyond the horizon.

But the struggle was always with him. Hunger never truly left, quietly gnawing at his stomach during those long nights when his mother had nothing more to give. The smell of the spice market was intoxicating, yet it served as a cruel reminder of the meals he could not afford.

The roasted cashews, golden samosas, and honey-drenched jalebis—these were all the delightful treats he could only dream of tasting. From a distance, he watched with his mouth watering as friendly traders wrapped goods in old newspapers and joyfully handed them to those fortunate enough to indulge. It was hard for him to accept that he wasn't among them.

Leo watched as alcohol took its toll on his father, feeling the weight of each moment. He noticed his mother's face tighten when Manuel staggered in and how her fingers trembled as she counted the few coins he hadn't spent. Leo could sense his father's anger flickering like unpredictable monsoon storms that sometimes battered their humble home. There were times filled with shouting, followed by long silences that made Leo's chest feel heavy.

The school was both a sanctuary and a difficult place to be. While the other boys had shiny shoes, neatly organised books, and lunches carefully packed in tin boxes, Leo only had his bare feet, a few borrowed notebooks, and a stomach that grumbled during lessons. Despite feeling like an outsider, he resolutely refused to let it define him. Knowledge became his weapon, shield, and route to a world beyond the spice market and the unending cycle of hardship.

The pursuit of a better quality of life often made the hardships feel even more intimidating. There were moments when hunger became almost too difficult to endure. There were nights when Leo lay awake, listening to the soft, quiet sobs of his mother, overwhelmed by a profound sense of helplessness. And, there were moments filled with uncertainty–gentle whispers in his mind that made him feel as though he were trapped in this life, as if escape were merely a distant dream.

Nevertheless, Leo held onto his beliefs with admirable strength. Leo refused to follow his father's path. He believed that obstacles were not burdens, but steps forward; each challenge was a chance to grow. With hope burning in him, he fixed his eyes on the future, leaving the past behind. Passionate and determined, he ran toward the life he believed he deserved.

The Night Everything Changed

The night Leo's father did not return home marked a significant turning point in Leo's childhood. The storm had been unrelenting for days, with fierce waves crashing against the docks, prompting the fishermen to exercise caution about going out to sea. Despite this, Manuel felt the weight of his debts pressing down on him, and in desperate times, it is often easy to ignore common sense.

From the very moment Elena woke up that morning, she sensed something was off, especially when she felt the coldness of the bed beside her. She just had this feeling that something was amiss. When they shared the news, she didn't burst into tears. Instead, she calmly wiped her hands on her apron, turning gently away from the neighbours' sympathetic glances and focusing back on kneading the dough. Leo stood by her side, watching to see if she would cry, get angry, or react in any way– but all she said was, "The sea does not return what it takes."

At fourteen, Leo realised that grief was a luxury they could not afford.

That night, the house felt cosier and more intimate. The walls seemed to embrace, creating a snug atmosphere, while the gentle glow of the oil lamp softly chased away the shadows, adding warmth to the quiet evening.

There was no funeral. No body to bury.

The sea had completely consumed Manuel, claiming him as its own. Instead, there were hushed voices, whispered condolences, and neighbours offering bowls of rice and lentils that they could barely afford themselves. They spoke in the same subdued tones usually reserved for discussing curses or misfortune, as though Manuel's death were contagious, as if they too harboured fears that the sea would claim their men next.

Elena barely acknowledged their presence. She moved through her small one-room house with a distant air, her hands constantly busy–washing, cooking, sweeping, keeping herself occupied to avoid moments of stillness. To her, quietness was a time for reflection that could evoke emotions and make her feel vulnerable, so she preferred to steer clear of such vulnerability.

Leo watched her with a mix of sorrow and confusion. He felt a strong urge to call out to her, to ask her to share her feelings and show that she cared, that she experienced the same pain he did. However, he held back. Instead, he remained seated at the wooden table, his eyes fixed on the empty chair where his father used to sit – the one that had held his father's gravelly voice as he shared tales of the sea, ships, storms, and dreams that seemed beyond their reach.

With Manuel Carlos's passing, the fragile veil of security that once offered comfort was permanently lifted, exposing a harsh, unwelcoming reality. The illusion of stability, already fragile, was entirely shattered. All that remained was a home filled with uncertainty and a family left to confront a world that no longer felt safe or reassuring. In the following days, a gentle, tangible silence filled the air. Grief seemed almost distant in this new chapter. There were no tears or long goodbyes; life pressed on with quiet resilience.

Each morning, Elena would wake up before sunrise, quietly slipping into the bakery while the town still slept. She found solace in her routine–kneading dough with care, her hands covered in flour. Each new day brought some blisters, gradually toughening her skin as the pain softened into something she could bear. Work became her safe haven, a warm place where she could temporarily set aside her grief, lost in the comforting rhythm of action and purpose.

Leo gradually realised a harsh truth: in a world weighed down by debt and peril, there is little room for sorrow. Manuel had been lost at sea, leaving behind no body to mourn–only unanswered questions and mounting responsibilities that ebbed like the tide, compelling the living to face them head-on.

Leo barely had time to process his loss before men started to appear–calm but intimidating figures who conveyed menace not just through their words but also in their silent presence. They arrived in pairs and small groups, each with their own name but united in purpose. Some were dressed sharply in tailored shirts, speaking with unsettling politeness, while others stood silently, their presence alone acting as a stark warning. What connected them all was their firm declaration: Manuel's debts now fell to Leo to handle. He realised they weren't ordinary men but part of a powerful network too strong to confront alone.

The demands kept coming, heavy and relentless. It was Elena who bravely greeted them at their door. When the knock sounded, she opened it with calm confidence. Standing upright with a resolute expression, she softly said, "Give me some time," her voice steady and assured, every word carefully chosen. She didn't ask for mercy or hesitate. The men exchanged glances and quietly departed. Leo felt that time was a precious gift they truly lacked.

They shared fleeting moments, like a family woven together by a shimmering thread of hope. Each day felt like a gentle negotiation, with every decision carefully weighed against the potential consequences. The rent deadline was approaching, creating a sense of urgency. The bakery's payments hadn't quite met expectations, and the fish market's kindness seemed to be waning. It almost felt as if the landlord's patience might run out soon, reminding everyone of the delicate balance they were all walking.

Leo carried a heavy burden on his shoulders, which sometimes made him feel overwhelmed. At only fourteen years old, he began to notice that his childhood was slowly slipping away, much like the peeling of a fruit, leaving him feeling vulnerable and exposed.

He watched his mother wake before dawn and go back to bed long after sunset. The concern was evident in the gentle lines of her face, and he noticed the slight tremors in her hands when she thought no one was looking. He also observed how her plate of food grew emptier each evening, as she made small excuses for her shrinking appetite, all just to give him another spoonful of rice.

He couldn't allow things to continue like this.

He learned the ways of the streets with eager zeal, happily running errands for local shopkeepers and carrying heavy sacks of rice alongside bright baskets of fresh vegetables. His small, hardworking hands grew calloused from the effort, but he took great pride in helping. At the market, he carefully cleaned fish, the salty scent clinging to his skin long after he finished. Sometimes, he would take small things–just a loaf of bread or some fruit to start. It was never much, but it was enough to ensure his beloved mother never went to bed hungry.

Elena never questioned where the extra food came from, but Leo knew she was aware. She simply sighed-a tired, broken sound–and let him believe he was fooling her, even if she understood the truth.

The nights proved to be quite challenging. The darkness was heavy, enveloping him from all sides, while the soothing sound of waves gently crashing against the shore created an atmosphere at once familiar and haunting. This scene reminded him of that unforgettable, stormy night and his father's absence. Over time, he developed a deep sense of disappointment towards the sea. It was hard for him to accept that it had taken so much without giving anything back, having swept his father away and left a void that seemed impossible to fill.

The uncertainty about their future felt like a looming storm cloud, casting a shadow over their daily lives. Each day was a struggle–facing hunger, dealing with financial worries, and questioning what tomorrow might bring. Leo found himself awake at night, staring at the ceiling, listening to the gentle rhythm of his mother's breathing, and pondering how much longer they could endure this together.

And then came the night when everything changed again.

It was late, and the streets were quiet and deserted, the city gently wrapped in the peaceful stillness of early morning. Leo was strolling back from the docks, having spent the evening helping a fisherman unload crate in exchange for some coins. He felt tired, with sore arms and a hungry stomach, when suddenly he heard them–voices, soft yet sharp, breaking the tranquillity of the night.

He crouched behind a pile of wooden crates, watching intently through the gaps. Two men stood by the bakery, their faces partly obscured beneath the flickering streetlamp. One was familiar–the landlord's son, known for his sinister grin and a tendency to resort to violence when debts remained unpaid. The other man was unfamiliar, but something about his appearance caused a sensation of unease in Leo.

They were talking about his mother.

"She's got a week," the landlord's son said. "If she can't pay, we take the house."

And what if she says no? the other man asked, his voice filled with light-hearted amusement.

Then we settle what's owed in another way.

Leo didn't need to hear more. As soon as the men spat their threats and mocked his mother, something inside him flared—an uncontrollable, fierce fire. His fists clenched at his sides, trembling, with nails digging into his palms so profoundly that he nearly drew blood. Rage filled his chest, sharp and blazing, blinding him with thoughts of revenge. He longed to scream, to attack, to make them fear him. But the harsh truth settled quickly and fiercely: he was just a boy. And they were grown men. Men like them didn't fear boys. They laughed at them, dismissed them, and broke them if necessary.

Leo turned and sprinted away. He hurried through the shadowy alleys, his footsteps banging on the dusty ground. His breathing was ragged, and his heart hammered fiercely. The tears he had been holding back earlier now pricked at the edges of his eyes, which he quickly wiped away in frustration, and a feeling of helplessness wrapped around.

When he burst through the door of their house, he saw Elena sitting quietly at the small wooden table. The candle beside her flickered softly, casting gentle shadows across the weary lines on her face. She didn't flinch when he suddenly entered. She looked up slowly, her eyes appearing slightly exhausted but still alert, always attentive, as if the worries of the world had taught her never to relax fully.

He spoke, his voice trembling with frustration and fury, revealing everything to her—how they talked, their harsh words, and hidden threats. He watched her carefully, expecting her to break down—perhaps tears, fear, or despair—but she didn't.

Elena gently closed her eyes, drawing a slow, calming breath. When she reopened them, her gaze revealed a quiet, unyielding determination.

"We leave," she said.

Leo stared, confused. "What?"

"We leave, Leo." Her voice sharpens, now steady with a kind of clarity he'd never heard from her before. "There's nothing left for us here—no safety, no future. We need to go before they can take any more from us."

He didn't speak, felt as if he couldn't. Instead, he looked at her and, perhaps for the first time, noticed the fire beneath her weariness. His mother—so tired, overworked, and grieving—wasn't giving up. She was choosing to fight, not with fists, but with her spirit. With a will to survive. In that moment, something beautiful shifted within Leo.

He nodded.

After a few days, they packed quietly, each movement full of gentle emotion. They didn't have much–just a few clothes, a small pouch of coins earned through years of effort, and a treasured photograph of Manuel, with softly folded corners revealing its age. Elena carefully tucked the picture into her blouse, holding it close to her heart. Their whole lives had been packed into a simple bundle that fit inside a worn cloth bag, but it carried far more significance.

As the sky slowly shifted from the peaceful quiet of night to the gentle glow of dawn, they slipped away quietly. The streets were calm, alive only with the soft chirping of birds and the distant sound of waves, creating a soothing backdrop. The town, which had been their beloved home–a place filled with childhood memories, laughter, and some bittersweet moments–gradually disappeared behind them with each step they took.

Leo and Liza were somewhat unsure about their destination. Elena hadn't shared any plans, and she might not have known either. Still, it wasn't crucial to them. What mattered most was staying together as a family and moving forward. They had left behind the quiet and were no longer waiting passively for trouble to catch up.

As they moved further away from the life that had once overwhelmed them, Leo looked at his mother–her chin held high despite being tired, and her hands steady despite her pain–and he felt a warm, comforting feeling grow inside him.

Although they had lost everything, being together remained a priceless gift that no debt collector, threat, or cruelty could ever take away.

On that day, he committed himself to something extraordinary—a pledge that seemed to become an intrinsic part of his identity.

They will never feel this helpless again.

Chapter 3
The Birth of the Fighter

A few years after moving to another coastal town in Goa, Leo found himself in his first real fight–not inside a boxing ring but behind a butcher's shop. A fist tore through the air before Leo even had time to think. He ducked, the blow grazing his ear, and swung back with raw instinct. Behind the butcher's shop, the night was alive with grunts, scuffling feet, and the metallic tang of blood that mixed with the stench of raw meat. There were no rules here–just two boys circling in the shadows, each strike a test of who would break first.

Leo realised that pain was only temporary, but humiliation lingered. He still remembered the time an older boy had slapped him in front of the spice sellers, sending him sprawling onto the dusty street as the crowd laughed. The sting on his cheek faded within minutes, but the echo of their laughter burned for weeks. From then on, he promised himself–he could take a punch, but he would never let himself be shamed again.

He learned to move with the rhythm of a fight, to slip past blows and flow back with his own. Losses came often at first, leaving him bruised and winded, but he refused to stay down. Each defeat only strengthened his resolve, sharpening his instincts. The first time his fist landed clean and accurate, sending his opponent stumbling, the rush was electrifying. In that moment, Leo wasn't just fighting–

he was learning what it meant to command a fight, and he knew he would pursue that mastery until it was his.

News spread quickly about the young man from the spice market, known for fists as strong as iron and a jaw that never wavered. At tea stalls, men leaned in over chipped glasses to share stories of how he had dropped a rival twice his size, while whispers circulated through narrow alleys where children mimicked his punches in play. Over the years, he steadily rose through the hidden fighting circles tucked into the city's backstreets, honing his skills in freestyle kickboxing. The bouts were brutal, the pay modest—but compared to his earlier life, it was still a step forward.

And then Lucas Dada came.

Lucas wasn't a fighter; he was a true kingmaker—a man whose reputation echoed through every alley and backroom where brawls occurred. He managed the city's largest underground fighting ring, a venue where higher stakes, more brutal clashes, and even greater rewards were at play. Fighters who earned his approval not only received financial benefits but also gained protection and a chance to escape the harsh struggles of the streets.

Leo had heard of him long before he saw him. The first time their paths crossed was after one of Leo's most brutal fights. He had defeated a seasoned brawler, a man twice his size, and was catching his breath when a slow clap echoed through the crowd.

Lucas stood at the edge of the makeshift ring, his tall figure cloaked in a dark coat. His face bore the marks of age, telling stories of the hardships he had endured. Still, his eyes remained bright, focused and contemplative.

"Not bad," Lucas said, his voice like gravel. "But not good enough."

Leo wiped the blood from his lip and stood up straight. "I won."

Lucas smirked. "Winning is just the beginning."

That evening, Leo was surprised to receive an invitation to join the underground fighting ring organised by Lucas. It was one of those invitations that couldn't be refused.

The warehouse where the fights took place felt quite different from the alleys and basements Leo knew so well. It was unexpectedly tidy and well-organised, which made everything seem even more dangerous - there was a sharp edge to the threat that went beyond mere physical harm. The people running the show weren't just gamblers; they were clever entrepreneurs involved in all sorts of activities, from smuggling to political dealings. And the fighters? They weren't just desperate souls trying to survive - they were genuine warriors, carefully chosen and thoroughly trained.

His debut fight in the underground circuit was against Bhaskar "Bones" More—a name that's often whispered with a mix of awe and caution in gym lockers and back-alley spots across Mumbai. For years, Bones moved through the city's shadowy fight scene like a ghost—unlicensed, unpredictable, and genuinely formidable. No one really knew where he came from, but everyone agreed that whenever he stepped into the ring, whether in an informal match or a formal one, he always turned it into a scene full of intense action.

Bones was more than a fighter; he embodied violence in its purest form.

They called him "Bones" not because of what he broke, but for what he left behind.

He had a commanding presence that could send shivers down your spine. His large frame bore the marks of years of street fights and prison brawls. Everyone recognised his fists—not for their size, but for the crushing strength they held. His knuckles, thick and weathered, bore scars like marks of former battles. Fighters said being hit by him was like being struck with a brick wrapped in skin—a real test of resilience.

But it wasn't the power—it was how he fought. No grace. No form. Just raw, relentless savagery. He didn't duck or weave. He absorbed punishment with a grimace and advanced like a freight train of pain. He grunted with every blow, sometimes laughed when he was hit. There were stories—unconfirmed, yet endlessly repeated—of him biting an opponent's ear mid-fight, of breaking a man's knee with one brutal stomp, and of ending a match by slamming his rival's face into a steel post.

Every injury Bones inflicted felt deeply personal.

His most notorious fight ended with his opponent convulsing on the mat, jaw shattered, ribs broken, and lung punctured. Bones left the scene blood-stained and smiling, as if he'd just finished a casual workout.

When Leo first saw him, Bones was pacing barefoot on the concrete, almost like a caged animal. His fierce gaze was fixed on Leo – not out of curiosity or respect, but with a hungry intensity. A sneer twisted his face, giving the impression that Leo was already broken, bleeding, and begging. The crowd roared around them, but Bones remained perfectly still. Instead, he slowly cracked his knuckles, one hand at a time, as if preparing for a skilful act of violence.

He entered alone, without any music or entourage, bearing only scars and an aura of menace. The underground audience revered him as a dark deity of suffering. In contrast, Leo was simply the next sacrifice, an upstart within this empire, an amateur, like a lamb led to slaughter.

Everyone watching that night understood one thing: when Bones stepped into the ring, something had to break. Most nights, it was bones. On the worst nights, it was men.

For Leo, this was a real test of resilience.

The crowd was bigger, livelier, and even more intense than any Leo had ever seen. The air was thick with the smells of sweat, alcohol, and a strong feeling of urgency. Spectators leaned against the rusted railings, waving bags of cash, shouting names loudly, swearing, and eager for a fight.

The bookmakers clearly showed their bias. Bets on Leo were predictably few–just small wagers from those supporting long shots. Most bets were on Bones. After all, Leo was the underdog, the outsider, the nobody–a young lad from Goa with only a few local wins to his name, facing a seasoned veteran who had left a trail of defeated opponents.

In the ring, bathed in the warm glow of the overhead bulbs, Leo felt the gentle weight of expectations—or perhaps just the tranquillity of their absence.

The fight began, and the referee gently reminded both fighters to shake hands. Bones wasted no time; he charged forward with the unstoppable energy of a freight train from the start. His fists swung with fierce determination, drawing cheers from the crowd. His style was full of passion, boldness, and raw power. Bones was eager to overpower Leo quickly, sending a clear message. Every punch was powerful, like a sledgehammer, narrowly missing Leo's skin and increasing the tense atmosphere of the match.

Leo's heart pounded, yet he stayed calm. He remembered Lucas Dada's words: "Survive the first storm, and the fight becomes yours."

So, he danced.

Unlike Bones, who fought with brute force and rage, Leo relied on timing and patience. His footwork skimmed the cracked concrete, light and fluid, as he slipped past wild punches. He let Bones burn himself out, always staying just beyond reach—dancing like a butterfly, elusive and untouchable. But beneath that grace coiled a hidden sting; Leo was waiting for the perfect moment to strike like a bee, calm and confident as the tension in the ring thickened with every near miss.

Bones snarled, "Stand still, you little shit!" But Leo kept moving, constantly circling and jabbing whenever he could. He didn't stay in one spot for more than a second, allowing Bones to tire himself out. He watched as Bones's breathing grew heavier, his footwork slowed, and his swings became wild and reckless.

By the end of the second round, Bones' chest was heaving like a wounded animal. While his punches still packed a punch, they seemed a bit less sharp than before.

That's when Leo made his move.

He slipped past the guard and quickly delivered a powerful left hook to the ribs, hearing the satisfying crack as Bones' air was forced out with a wheeze. The crowd gasped in amazement as the momentum suddenly shifted.

Leo advanced confidently, landing two strong body shots and a swift uppercut that jerked Bones' head backwards, causing sweat to spray like mist under the bright arena lights.

In the third round, Bones came in aggressively again, now desperate, swinging wildly. Leo sidestepped, planted his feet, and delivered a brutal right cross straight to the jaw. The sound of it echoed through the mill—meat and bone colliding with grim finality.

Bones staggered, eyes glassy, legs buckling. Leo didn't hesitate for a moment. With determination, he delivered a final, merciless left hook that struck him squarely on the temple.

Bones crumpled like a felled tree, hitting the mat with a loud thud. The referee started the count, but everyone knew it was over.

Leo stood there, with his chest heaving and arms raised–not in celebration, but in defiance. Blood slowly trickled from a cut on his brow, yet his eyes shone with a fierce determination. He wasn't merely fighting the monster before him–he was standing up against a world that had misunderstood and wronged him.

The underdog had triumphed. In that moment, Leo wasn't just standing over Bones; he was standing over every doubt that had ever shadowed him, every sneer that had mocked his hunger, every whisper that tied him to his father's debts.

The crowd paused briefly, seemingly absorbing the shocking turn of events. Then, quite suddenly, they erupted into cheers–some filled with awe, others a little disappointed about their lost bets. But for Leo, the lively noise around him faded into a soft background. The only sounds he could truly hear were the pounding of his heart and the triumphant roar echoing inside him.

From that night onwards, Leo Carlos was no longer a kid from the streets. He was a fighter, and the underground scene took notice.

Lucas was watching.

The fights became more frequent, and the stakes increased even further. With each bout, Leo's reputation spread rapidly through the alleys and backstreets of Goa. He was no longer just an ordinary street fighter; he had become a serious contender.

But success was a double-edged sword. It attracted the kind of attention he never desired–dangerous attention.

Rival fighters weren't just trying to beat Leo–they sought to wipe his presence from the underground fighting scene entirely. His swift and impressive rise made him a target for envy and resentment. They hurled threats across sweaty gym floors, followed him into alleyways after matches, and whispered promises of broken bones and lost pride. Some played mind games to get into his head, while others resorted to dirty tactics in the ring–elbows to the back of the head, punches after the bell, and spitting in his face to provoke a reaction.

But Leo offered them nothing. He remained calm, focused, and constantly thought ahead. He didn't let feelings influence his judgment. Fame no longer mattered to him. Every fight was about survival, about getting through another night, another breath. In the brutal world of blood sport and ego, Leo's true strength wasn't just his fists–it was his discipline. Staying composed became his armour, silence his way of standing tall, and survival his peaceful revenge.

And then there were the ones who didn't even bother playing fair.

It was late—another night soaked in monsoon drizzle, with the city shimmering with oil and grime. Leo was walking home after a fight that had left the crowd cheering for more, his body still buzzing with adrenaline and a sense of victory.

He slipped into a familiar, narrow alley shortcut he'd taken countless times before. But tonight, something felt a little different, a bit off.

A shadow ahead shifted uneasily, unlike the usual drunkard or beggar. It had the nervous, jittery movements of someone waiting for him, heightening the scene's tense and personal atmosphere.

Leo came to a sudden halt, instincts roaring.

In just an instant, he saw a figure rush out of the darkness, a knife gleaming under the streetlamp's dull yellow light.

Leo narrowly dodged. The knife ripped through his sleeve, the cold edge grazing his skin and leaving a thin line of fire in its wake. His breath caught—too close. For a heartbeat, the blade hovered between them, the attacker's grip iron-tight, knuckles straining. Leo felt the pulse in his wrist, pounding against time. Then instinct surged. His hand shot out, clamping onto the man's wrist. He twisted hard, tendons grinding beneath his grip, until the knife juddered free and clattered to the ground. The man yelped, but Leo's eyes were still locked on the threat, his body coiled for the next move.

A second attacker sneaked up from behind. Leo quickly spun around and elbowed him sharply in the ribs, causing him to gasp for air. The man doubled over, coughing and wheezing as he attempted to regain his breath.

They were not fighters; they were amateurs–hired muscle brought in by someone aiming to eliminate Leo... quickly.

He left them writhing in the gutter.

But the message was unmistakably clear.

The next day, he found a note in his locker at the gym where he trained.

"Watch your back."

Leo wasn't naive. He knew how the game was played.

He trained more diligently, honing each skill and refining every weakness. He began to observe and listen attentively. He became aware of those who lingered near the betting tables, noted which faces reacted when specific names were mentioned, and discerned who engaged in whispered conversations in back rooms before matches.

He realised that the fighters weren't the only ones involved in the game. The real power was hidden behind the scenes, within the shadows. The people in suits, who never stepped into the ring, held the true control, deciding who would rise and who would fall. They had their fingers in every part of the process–manipulating matches before the first bell, controlling the bets, managing the flow of money, and overseeing the risks. It was a concealed world running the show from behind the scenes.

And Leo had become more than just a fighter.

He was a player.

A dangerous one.

He would fight. He would win.

But now, he was ready to do even more. He'd uncovered the secret behind the game. And one day, when the moment was right, he'd make the entire city play by his rules.

Chapter 4
Devil in a Suit

Lucas Dada's journey is truly inspiring. As a boy, Lucas darted through the crowded lanes of Goa, weaving past vendors and fishermen, learning early how to survive on his wits. Years later, those same streets no longer swallowed him—they echoed his name with fear. His original name might have faded into the background, overshadowed by the bustling streets he once explored, but it has become part of the legend he's carefully built. To those who knew him as a child, he was simply an ordinary young boy navigating the busy streets of Panaji, always eager for new opportunities. Today, he is recognised as an influential figure in the criminal world – a name spoken with caution, bearing a desire for revenge that can even turn paradise into chaos.

His empire was truly greater than most could envision. From the opulent casinos along the Mandovi River to the clandestine smuggling routes crossing the coastal borders, everything appeared centred around him. Law enforcement officials turned a blind eye to these activities, having been paid generous sums in untraceable cash. Politicians at charitable events acted kindly, while secretly aware that their campaigns thrived thanks to their discreet backing. Even rival gangs understood that it was wiser not to challenge his control openly.

Lucas Dada wasn't just a crime boss; he was an institution in his own right.

In the world Leo was entering, power wasn't simply handed out; it was seized fiercely, with careful planning and bravado. Those who waited for permission remained at the bottom, while those daring enough to take it, understanding that control often demanded strategic force, rose up.

Lucas Dada was the perfect example.

Lucas didn't just inherit his empire–he built it from the ground up, with hands that had weathered many battles and a heart shaped by hard streets. His story, whispered across Goa's underground, began with a single, brave act of fierce determination.

The altercation started over what seemed to be a trivial matter: a card game. At that time, Lucas was an aspiring hustler eager for success. Sadly, he had been misled by Ramesh Patil, a ruthless card sharp known for his toughness and notorious for sneering at those he considered inferior. When Lucas saw Patil fiddling with the deck, he decided to confront him, perhaps a little naive and bold, but still committed to his principles of fair play.

Patil's laughter rang out with a sharp, scornful tone, his eyes gleaming with contempt. He stepped closer, smirking, and subtly pointed a finger at his chest. "Go on," he said with a sneer, "try to do something." The challenge lingered in the air, playfully daring him, taunting his silence, and igniting the fire within.

Without hesitation, he grabbed the nearest thing he could–a broken beer bottle and swung it hard at Patil's throat. Patil staggered back, choking, his eyes bulging as a wet gasp rattled out, before he crumpled face-first onto the filthy backroom floor, lifeless.

That evening, Lucas learned two lessons that would eventually shape his character.

Firstly, fear wielded a far greater influence than respect ever could. Secondly, in such a world, hesitation, doubt, or even a hint of mercy was seen as a sign of weakness–chinks in the armour that could be pretty dangerous.

From that moment onwards, Lucas never hesitated again.

As he advanced through the ranks, Lucas built a formidable reputation that seemed nearly unstoppable. He surrounded himself with individuals who inspired more fear than even death itself. His enforcers weren't merely troublemakers; they were loyal followers of his beliefs. If anyone refused to pay protection fees, their businesses would be entirely destroyed. If a rival tried to seize his territory, their bodies would later be washed up, unrecognisable and decomposed. Lucas didn't just send messages–he issued warnings carved into flesh and bone.

Despite his fierce reputation, Lucas Dada was more than just a brute. He had a remarkable talent for understanding people, often recognising their weaknesses before they even realised it themselves. He was patient and strategic, carefully building alliances and waiting for the perfect moment to act.

Goa's vibrant tourism scene was like his personal playground, shining brightly with wealth and luxury, while concealing a hidden undercurrent of crime. The high rollers at his casinos revelled in their winnings without a second thought, and the smugglers using his ports didn't question what else might be passing through.

His influence was truly significant and unmistakable.

As soon as a new business opened in Goa, Lucas somehow knew—often even before the ink on the contracts had dried. His extensive network was well-connected with local authorities, law firms, and even political circles. A simple whisper was enough. Before the owners could even celebrate their launch, they would receive a subtle visit or a cryptic message—Lucas's way of signalling that in Goa, nothing happened without his knowledge.

He had eyes everywhere—hotel staff, taxi drivers, and even street vendors. Information was his true currency, and he exchanged it deftly. When foreign drug cartels attempted to enter his territory, they found themselves mysteriously detained, their operations dismantled before they could establish themselves. Some whispered that Lucas had informants within the upper echelons of law enforcement, ensuring that Goa remained his uncontested domain.

Yet, despite his dominance, some still aspired to overthrow him. The younger gangs, ambitious and reckless, occasionally dared to challenge him.

They repeatedly failed.

Lucas had a natural talent for turning challenges into lessons, and those lessons were often painful for others. When Raghu, a brave gangster from the outskirts, tried to take over Lucas's smuggling routes, it was apparent it wouldn't just be a simple dispute. Raghu was young, confident, and believed he could dominate part of the coastal trade by undercutting prices. However, he didn't realise how skilled Lucas truly was. There were no warnings or negotiations. Just swift, decisive action.

One night, Raghu vanished. Word spread that Lucas's men had snatched him off the streets, tossing him into the boot of an unmarked car. They dragged him to an abandoned dockyard on the outskirts of Vasai, where the only witnesses were rusted shipping containers and the dark sea. They didn't shoot him. His men beat Raghu to death slowly, methodically, leaving his broken body hanging from a crane hook as a message.

Lucas, despite any fears he might evoke, was far from being a monster. To those he trusted, he was known as a man of integrity who always kept his promises. Loyalty meant a great deal to him, and he was quick to reward it. His principles were somewhat complex–more than just about morality, they also involved maintaining complete control. While he despised betrayal, he also avoided unnecessary killings, revealing a more layered side of himself.

To outsiders, however, his fury appeared as random brutality, chaos devoid of order. But those who knew him understood the truth. Every move was deliberate, and each death served a reason.

It was after a fierce fight that Lucas spoke to Leo. The warehouse was dimly lit, and the air was thick with sweat and the metallic tang of blood. Leo stood victorious, his knuckles bruised, and his opponent sprawled unconscious at his feet. The other men watched silently, wary of what was to come. Lucas stepped forward, dressed in his signature crisp white shirt, with a gold watch gleaming beneath the flickering lights.

"You fight like a man with something to prove," Lucas observed, his voice calm yet carrying an unmistakable weight.

Leo met his gaze, defiant but not foolish. "Maybe I do."

"Good. But strength without direction is wasted energy," Lucas said, his voice smooth and deliberate. "You have fists, but I can give you purpose."

The words struck something raw in Leo. Part of him burned to spit back, to prove he didn't need anyone's guidance. But another part–tired of alleyway scraps, of fighting only to survive–felt the pull of what Lucas promised. Purpose. The chance to matter. The temptation coiled inside him, dangerous and undeniable, even as his pride warned him not to bend.

That was Lucas Dada. A man who recognised potential and forged the reckless into weapons for his empire. He was a kingmaker. And in the world, he created, there was no room for weakness–only power.

Leo understood what he meant. Working for Lucas was a trade-off between morality and power. Choosing a life where the rules were flexible, where survival was about conquering rather than simply living.

He opted for power.

The initiation was not a handshake or a signature on paper. It was an act of submission—one that made Leo realise exactly what he was becoming.

Lucas had assigned him a name, a target: a small-time bookie who had refused to pay his cut. "Remind him," Lucas had said with a smile that didn't reach his eyes. "Make sure he never forgets."

Leo found the man in a dilapidated flat above a tailor's shop. He was older, balding, with a face etched with fear before Leo had even made contact. "Please," the man had pleaded, "I need a little more time."

Leo hesitated. A fight was one thing. This was different.

Then he recalled the hunger, the nights he had spent curled up in alleyways, the pain of loss. Lucas had rescued him from that. And there was no turning back now.

The first punch shattered the man's nose. The second broke his ribs. By the time Leo was finished, the bookie lay on the ground, whimpering, choking on his own blood. Leo left without a word, his knuckles raw, his heart heavier than he wanted to admit.

When he returned, Lucas was waiting, sipping whisky in his private lounge above the fight ring. "How did it feel?" he asked.

Leo didn't answer.

Lucas chuckled. "Don't lie to yourself, kid. Power is a drug. The first taste always burns, but soon enough, you'll crave it."

The words sank deep into Leo's chest. A part of him bristled, wanting to dismiss it as manipulation–but the truth was, he did remember the burn, the intoxicating rush of his first real victory. The memory made his pulse quicken. He feared Lucas might be right, worried that hunger was already in him, waiting to be fed.

Over the years, Leo continued to progress, moving into larger venues with even greater rewards, although he also encountered more challenges along the way. But fighting was just one part of his story. Lucas also began exploring other ways to support his goals–such as using intimidation, enforcement, and ensuring things stayed quiet when necessary.

One night, Lucas called him in for a special task.

"A journalist is sniffing around," he said, sliding a photograph across the table. "She's asking questions she shouldn't be asking."

Leo looked at the photograph. A woman in her late thirties had sharp eyes and a determined jawline. Not a fighter. Not a gangster. But a woman doing her job.

"Scare her," Lucas ordered. "Make her understand that curiosity is dangerous."

Leo spotted her outside a café, walking alone. He followed her for a few blocks, slipping into the alleys and waiting patiently for the right moment.

Then he saw her stop, pull out her phone, and dial a number.

"I think I'm being followed," she said into the receiver, her voice full of fear.

Leo clenched his fists, feeling a surge of determination. He could almost see the scene unfolding–him stepping forward, gently grasping her arm, and softly warning her in a way that might make her reconsider her investigation. He noticed the fear in her eyes, the way she instinctively pulled back, feeling helpless yet also aware of his presence.

He could see himself turning into exactly what Lucas had moulded him to be.

He paused briefly, then gently turned around and selected a different route, as if opting for an alternative path.

The next day, she was dead.

The newspaper described it as a tragic hit-and-run. But Leo knew better. Lucas's influence was extensive, and his punishments were definitive.

At the boxing ring that night, Lucas greeted him with a knowing smile. "You hesitated," he said.

Leo remained silent.

Lucas leaned in, his voice nearly tender. "Don't make that mistake again."

It was more than just a threat; it was a promise, delivered with a confident and assured tone.

Leo acknowledged this reality with a nod, but deep down, he felt a strong sense of disillusionment. For the first time, he realised that power was not a gift bestowed by Lucas; instead, it was something to be seized—gradually.

Chapter 5
The Price of Power

Working for Lucas felt like entering a world where everything was different, and moral boundaries sometimes seemed like a luxury too far for many. Leo quickly recognised this. At first, his tasks were simple – delivering parcels, collecting debts, and ensuring people paid what they owed. But as he gained confidence and influence, he began craving more. Soon, Leo evolved from a street fighter into Lucas's trusted enforcer, the one sent to deliver messages–sometimes with a firm touch.

He didn't intend for things to become this intense. At least, that's what he kept telling himself. There's always a reason, an excuse. The first incident involved a man who refused to pay his debt, spat at Leo's feet, and laughed while he tried to reason with him. The second involved someone who stole from Lucas–stole from all of them. That's how Lucas saw it, saying, "We're a family, Leo. And a family doesn't let betrayal slide."

A family. The word might have felt empty now, but Leo wanted to believe in it then. He longed to think that his actions were necessary, that he was more than just someone breaking bones for money. He convinced himself he was different, that he had control over things. But control is only an illusion, and Leo was too caught up to see it.

His mother was aware.

She had a remarkable talent for noticing what others might overlook. She spotted the bruises that didn't match the fight reports—those that seemed too detailed, too angry. She paid attention to how his shoulders would hunch even when he wasn't in the ring, and how his hands would curl into fists during sleep, as if he was bracing himself for something he couldn't escape. She also listened at night—the sharp breaths, the muffled groans, the restless tossing. A mother knows when her child is troubled or haunted.

She tried to reach out to him with a gentle approach. As her emotions grew stronger, she spoke through tears. In the end, she fell silent. But Leo had already sunk deeper into darkness. The underground circuit had taken control of him. The money, the blood, the feeling of power—they enveloped him like smoke, hard to escape.

"I know what you're doing, Leo," she said one evening. She stood in the kitchen, backlit by the amber glow of a single bulb, her voice heavy with sorrow and fatigue. "I see it in your face. You think this is the only way, but it's not."

Leo didn't look at her. He stood by the sink, hands beneath the running tap, watching the water change from murky red to clear. His knuckles were raw, and his fingernails were caked with blood and grime.

"You don't understand," he muttered, his voice low, almost ashamed. "This is all I've got."

His mother moved closer, her arms folded tightly across her chest. "That's a lie you tell yourself. You've always had more than this."

"You don't understand," Leo muttered, avoiding her gaze as he rinsed his hands under the tap. The water flashed red for a moment before swirling down the drain.

"Then explain it to me," she pressed. "Explain why my son comes home looking like a man I don't recognise."

Nevertheless, there were no explanations that could truly justify it. No words could undo what he had done. So, he chose to stay silent, allowing the weight of her disappointment to hang between them, like an insurmountable wall.

Liza had always been his greatest supporter. From the joyful days of racing through narrow alleys and inventing games in their childhood, they dreamed of more – of a future where they wouldn't just scrape by but truly flourish, with plenty of food and a place they could call home. Now, as the city sprawls beneath them in a glowing haze of neon and endless opportunities, she still holds onto the hope that her brother can find his own way forward.

They gathered close on the road outside, feeling the warm, humid night air around them. The gentle, distant sounds of traffic provided a soft background. The city lights twinkled nearby, and beyond that, the casinos shimmered with an alluring glow–set apart from their world, tempting with promises of wealth but offering little real value to people like them.

"Is this really who you want to be?" Liza's voice was gentle, almost carried away by the breeze, yet her words cut through the silence between them with clarity.

She gently drew her knees up to her chest, her eyes softly fixed on Leo, quietly searching his face for the brother she once knew and cherished.

Leo didn't answer immediately. He looked out at the city, mesmerised by the shimmering casinos, with his jaw clenched in a way that made him seem wiser beyond his years.

"I want more than this, Liza," he said softly, his voice gentle and low. "I dream of a life where we don't have to beg, where we're not forced to watch Mama work so hard just for scraps."

Liza's eyes subtly softened, but she stayed resolute. "Respect and fear aren't the same thing, Leo," she said quietly.

He scoffed, his voice tinged with a hint of bitterness. "You think I don't know that?"

"Do you?" she asked, turning fully to face him. Her eyes–so like their mother's–gleamed with a hard intensity in the moonlight. "I watch how people look at you, Leo. It isn't admiration I see. It's caution. Wariness. That isn't respect. And it isn't what we dreamed of in our childhood."

Leo clenched his fists, the muscles in his forearms tense. He looked away, unable to meet her eyes. "It doesn't matter," he muttered.

"It should," she insisted, her voice trembling with emotion. "It matters to me. I don't care what you've done or how far you think you've gone. You're still my brother.

But I'm scared, Leo. I'm scared of what you're becoming. Of what you might lose if you keep going down this path."

He sat in silence, her words weighing down on him, heavy and relentless, as if the air itself had thickened. For a long moment, all that could be heard was the distant hum of the city, with the world continuing to move beneath them.

Liza reached out, her hand gentle on his arm. "You're better than this. I know you are. Please, Leo. Don't let this place change you into someone you're not."

He gently closed his eyes, sensing her touch as a comforting anchor. For the first time in a long while, Leo quietly began to believe that he might find his way back. As they sat together under the shimmering stars, the bond they shared remained strong, shining as his last and most hopeful chance for redemption.

For a moment, he wanted to believe her. He wished he could still change, that there was a way out. But Lucas didn't let people go. Not unless they were in a body bag.

A week later, Leo stood over another man, his knuckles sore and bloodstained. The man groaned and tried to crawl away, but Leo gently grasped his shirt collar and softly pulled him back. His heart was pounding rapidly, and he wasn't sure if it was from adrenaline or something even more terrifying deep inside.

Lucas stood nearby, watching calmly. "That's enough," he said softly, his voice steady and composed. Leo relaxed his grip, stepping back as the man sank to the ground, coughing gently.

Lucas gently patted Leo on the shoulder with a warm smile. “See? That wasn’t so hard.”

Leo swallowed the bile rising in his throat and nodded, feeling a sense of relief. He had met expectations and fulfilled his purpose.

That night, he sat alone at home, staring at his bruised knuckles. Liza’s words echoed in his mind. Is this truly who you want to be?

He didn’t know anymore.

The next day, he paused to watch his mother before leaving. She remained by the entrance, looking at him with that same caring concern she had recently shown–like someone deeply worried about the man he's becoming.

“You can still walk away, Leo,” she said softly.

He paused briefly, then shook his head and said, “Not anymore.”

Her eyes reflected a deep emotion that he found almost too difficult to face, so he quietly turned away and stepped back into the world he had deliberately embraced–a world where power came with its own price, and he was ready to bear it.

Chapter 6
A New Beginning

That night, Leo underwent a profound change. At first, it was just a faint sensation–a whisper in his mind. But as he lay awake in the suffocating silence of his flat, it grew stronger, tugging at his thoughts. The faint streetlamp light seeped through broken blinds, casting distorted shadows on the ceiling. He traced their shapes with tired eyes, watching them shift into different forms–Elena's weary smile, Liza's sharp suspicion, Lucas's calculating stare. These shadows flickered and moved, refusing to remain still, much like his confidence. What once seemed confident–his loyalty, ambition, and trust in Lucas–now appeared fragile, delicate, ready to break. This sensation clawed at him, blending fear and awakening, prompting him to question whether the life he was building was truly his... or just a prison concealed by power.

The streets had been his home, his battleground, and his prison. They had shaped him, hammered him, and reforged him into someone almost unrecognisable. Violence was the only language he knew, survival his only creed. Yet on this evening, as he allowed himself a rare moment of stillness, the truth struck–he was trapped. Not only by Lucas, who pulled his strings like a puppet master, but by the weight of his own choices. The cage was of his own making: the decisions he had made, the identity he had built, and the monster he had permitted himself to become.

He gently turned onto his side and closed his eyes, hoping for a peaceful sleep, but it just wouldn't come. His body still ached, and his knuckles remained swollen from earlier, adding to his discomfort.

He could hear the gentle hum of the city outside—sounds like the distant roar of an engine and the fading echoes of laughter that softly drift into the night. Somewhere out there, life carried on with its vibrant energy. People were living freely, without the constant pull of fear, and there was no need to look over their shoulders. He found himself contemplating what that kind of life truly was—what it felt like to wake up in the morning without the weight of blood on one's hands.

Leo's mother's voice echoed tenderly in his mind, a cherished memory from long ago. "You don't have to be like this, Leo. You're better than this."

Back then, he laughed it off, acting as if it wasn't a big deal. But in hindsight, it was more significant than he realised—especially now. He sometimes wished he had paid more attention and taken a moment to pause before everything spiralled out of control. Still, he wondered—was it truly too late? That question kept nagging at him, brighter than ever.

He thought of Liza, remembering how she looked at him that night - her eyes shining with a mix of sadness and hope. She had seen something in him that he no longer recognised. Was it even possible for him to become that person again? Could he find a way to climb out of the hole he had been digging for years?

Lucas refused to allow anyone to leave, knowing that if he escaped, he would be pursued. In Lucas's world, there was no safety net or second chances. He had witnessed the consequences for those attempting to escape, but he also observed the effects on those who stayed – their identities fading, violence becoming normal, and guilt turning into indifference. He no longer wished to face such a fate.

The clock on the wall ticked away seconds, each feeling longer than the last. The atmosphere in the flat felt stifling, pressing down on his chest and making it hard to breathe. He swung his legs off the bed, placing his feet on the cold wooden floor. His heart pounded as he reached for the duffel bag in the corner – the one he had packed during a moment of uncertainty. He had never used it, as he lacked the necessary resolve. However, tonight felt markedly different.

He moved swiftly and instinctively, opening drawers and grabbing the small amount of cash he had hidden away. He packed a few clothes, along with a faded old photograph of his mother and Liza. As he looked at the picture, he hesitated, gently running his thumb over its worn edges. Would they understand why he was leaving? Would they forgive him for everything he had done?

A deep breath. In. Out. He zipped the bag shut and threw it over his shoulder with finality. He looked around the apartment one last time–the cracked walls, the flickering kitchen light, and the pile of unpaid bills sitting on the counter–all reminders of his past. This place had kept him confined, but now he was ready to embrace a new beginning.

As he reached for the door, his pulse quickened with a mixture of anticipation and nerves. He knew this was the most dangerous moment. Lucas had his eyes on him, making it vital to remain calm. If they noticed him leaving or if suspicion was raised, everything could collapse. He gently turned the knob and stepped into the silent corridor. The building was still, apart from the soft hum of a television behind one of the doors, adding a touch of normality. He moved swiftly, muscles tense but prepared to run if necessary.

The cool night air wrapped around him as he stepped outside, softly brushing against his skin. He kept his head bowed, lost in thought, walking with quiet purpose but at a slow pace. The streets were bustling, filled with the sounds of vehicles and the hum of people laughing, talking, and going about their lives. Although he'd been among them for years, he often felt like an outsider, a ghost gently drifting through the world. Yet tonight, a surprising feeling of freedom washed over him for the first time in ages.

Or so he thought.

A voice pierced the noise. "Leo."

His blood ran cold.

He slowly turned, his heart pounding with anticipation. From the shadows, a figure emerged, cigarette smoke drifting softly through the air. It was a familiar face– one of Lucas's men. The look in his eyes was knowing, with a touch of amusement, making the moment feel even more emotionally charged.

"Going somewhere?"

Leo tightened his grip on the strap of his duffel bag as his thoughts began to whirl. He could tell himself he was just heading out for a quick drink, but deep down, he knew that wouldn't really fool them. They knew him too well, after all. They'd been watching him closely. Yes, they certainly had.

He could fight, if necessary, but he knew that doing so could only attract more unwanted attention. Once that happened, Lucas would discover what was going on well before he had a chance to escape the city.

Or he could run.

The man took a step forward. "You know how this goes, Leo. Nobody walks away."

Leo's jaw clenched. His fingers twitched at his side. He felt his past closing in around him like a noose.

But something had shifted, and he wouldn't be returning.

Without saying another word, he turned and ran.

Leo sat up straight, taking deep, shaky breaths as his heart pounded within his chest. For a moment, the dream still clung to him like smoke, with its images refusing to let go. Then, with a jolt, the world shifted–the muffled honk of a scooter, the rattle of a passing truck, the faint call of a street vendor–all of it crashing in simultaneously. The sudden noise tore him out of the haze, snapping the thread of the dream and pulling him back to reality.

The soft glow from the streetlamp outside filtered through the cheap blinds, casting playful, stretching shadows on the walls of his small, cosy flat. The sheets beneath him felt damp with sweat and clung uncomfortably to his skin. He gently ran a trembling hand through his wet hair, trying to calm himself, though the pounding in his chest still persisted, reminding him of his unease.

The nightmare still haunted him, its images clear and overwhelming.

The blood, the screams, and the vacant look in the eyes of the person he had left broken on the ground haunted his mind. The way Lucas later smiled at him, patting him on the shoulder like a proud father, was chilling. Years had passed since that first night, but the memory had not faded. If anything, it had grown more vivid, like a blade he had never learned to put down.

He reflected on his first encounter with Lucas; Leo was eager to prove his worth and demonstrate his value. Lucas recognised this strong desire and the innate need to belong, choosing to take Leo under his wing. At first, it felt like a welcome relief–Lucas gave him a sense of purpose, authority, and a place in the world. However, as time passed, the weight of the power he held began to feel heavier. Each act of violence, every life impacted, and every bridge burnt drew him closer to where he is now.

Leo shifted on the bed, the worn mattress softly creaking beneath him. His body was battered from the bruises sustained in recent fights and the heavy toll of years marked by violence. He closed his eyes, but sleep refused to come. His mind kept replaying the events of the night before—Lucas's threats, the possessive looks in his eyes, and the uneasy flutter in Leo's stomach that made him feel as if freedom was just out of reach.

But why? Why had he allowed it to go on for so long? Why had he let the streets shape him? He once believed he had no choice, thinking this was his fate. Kids like him—abandoned, broken, desperate—seemed to have nowhere else to turn. Yet now, he finds himself uncertain. Perhaps he has always had a choice, but fear has kept him from taking it.

His humble home held memories of a past that no longer felt like his own. The firearm on the nightstand caught the faint light, a silent witness to every choice he couldn't take back. How many times had he raised it without hesitation? How often had he convinced himself it was necessary, even righteous? Now, as his fingers hovered over the cold steel, it seemed to drag at him, heavier than metal should be—like it carried the sum of his sins.

His throat tightened, and his grip on the gun weakened momentarily.

He reflected on the people he had hurt and how his actions had unexpectedly changed lives forever. Although he had served as a soldier for Lucas and been a loyal enforcer, he couldn't shake the question of what he might have sacrificed–his soul? His humanity? This realisation made him feel truly uneasy. For years, he relied on his strength and independence to deal with his circumstances, but now, everything seemed to have shifted, feeling different and more uncertain.

But in truth, he had been a pawn, just another piece in Lucas's game. And now, he wanted to escape.

Leo finally allowed himself to imagine a different life–one free from violence, fear, and Lucas's shadow. He pictured leaving everything behind and starting afresh. Yet, he couldn't help but wonder: was such a dream even possible? Would Lucas truly let him go? Deep down, he already knew the answer. No one ever managed to escape Lucas–at least, not while they were still alive.

A chill ran down his spine as a wave of coldness seeped through his veins like icy water. If he were to escape, he knew he would have to fight for it. He needed to be clever, strategic, and resolute. After years of playing Lucas's game, he was finally ready to take control and play his own.

His heart pounded faster, a steady rhythm of both anxiety and resolve. Retreat was not an option. Lucas had eyes everywhere, his influence stretching across the entire city. As soon as he uncovered Leo's plans, he would strike like a fierce storm–swift and relentless. Leo understood he had to devise a clever plan. He needed something to gain an advantage. Most importantly, he required the courage to see it through.

The atmosphere in his room felt a bit heavier that night, with the walls almost closing in, creating a tight, suffocating sensation like an iron vice. He paced back and forth, his fists clenched and unclenched at his sides, feeling the tension in his fingers and the ache in his jaw from grinding his teeth. All those years of loyalty and service had built up inside him like a dam, and now, cracks were beginning to show. The flood of resentment, fear, and desperate hope was very close to overwhelming him.

He had endured many years of despair, suffocating under Lucas's control. He watched friends disappear, seeing the terror in their eyes just before they fell into the void. He learned to stay inconspicuous, follow orders, and ignore the cries in the night. He had become emotionally numb.

But something had changed, and it felt like a new beginning.

Perhaps it was the way Lucas looked at him now–like a dog that had outlived its usefulness. Or maybe it was the creeping fear of betrayal, with paranoia gently filling each interaction. It could also be the realisation that, no matter how loyal he remained, he might never truly feel completely safe.

Or perhaps he was just weary.

Weary of the blood. Weary of the fear. Weary of living like a man with a knife constantly pressed against his throat.

Leo took a deep breath, trying to steady himself. He realised he couldn't let fear hold him back any longer. After many years of avoiding the truth and himself, he was finally ready to face it. He made his decision with a renewed sense of resolve.

He was determined to escape the drudgery and suffering, to carve out a life where his mother and sister could live in peace, with the dignity and respect they deserved.

The plan started as a quiet thought at the back of his mind, just a faint idea that gradually took shape. He needed financial resources, a way to escape, and most importantly, a strategic advantage.

He spent nights in darkness, lost in thought, trying to imagine all the possibilities and reviewing every chat he had with Lucas. He wondered what weaknesses he might exploit and who he could truly trust. The answers came slowly and painfully, almost as if his mind was resisting the idea of breaking free.

Later that evening, as he sat alone and gazed at the illuminated skyline, a realisation struck him.

Lucas harboured secrets. Secrets potent enough to ruin him. And Leo knew where to locate them.

The warehouse was on the eastern side of town, the one Lucas always kept locked, the one no one was permitted to approach.

Leo's stomach churned as he realised what he had to do. It was suicide, a fool's errand. Yet it was also his only chance.

He grasped the steering wheel tightly, his knuckles whitening with effort. His heart thumped loudly in his ears, but beneath his fear, there was a quiet, stirring sense of resolve. Rage.

The years of pain and struggle, giving in to Lucas's wishes, and losing parts of himself–all the wounds, scars, and restless nights flooded back like a powerful wave, washing away the doubts.

Lucas had taken everything from him.

Now, was the time to reclaim everything.

—

The night carried a restless weight, every breath laced with the scent of danger, as if something was about to break. Leo moved silently through the city's hidden corners, every sense heightened by adrenaline and a sense of urgency. He had been waiting for this moment, prepared for it, and now that it was here, the weight of what he was about to do felt almost overwhelming. Staying in the shadows, he crept along the cracked pavement, his heart racing with a mix of fear and excitement.

The warehouse loomed ahead, a vast shadow against the overcast sky. It was a place often spoken of in hushed tones, a fortress where Lucas concealed the remnants of his crumbling empire. Leo's breath formed clouds in the chilly air as he leaned against the wall, carefully watching for any signs of movement. The silence was only broken by the distant hum of traffic and the gentle lapping of water against the docks. He took a deep, calming breath, trying to keep his hands from trembling.

He retrieved a set of lockpicks from his pocket– skills born of survival, not desire. The lock was old and stubborn, but Leo's hands were steady and his mind alert. Each click echoed like a heartbeat, steady and deliberate, pulling him closer to the truth. When the final tumbler gave way, the door creaked open, and he slipped inside, consumed by the waiting darkness.

The air was cool and slightly stuffy, filled with the subtle scent of oil and hidden secrets. Leo flicked on his torch, its narrow beam softly piercing the darkness.

What he saw took his breath away–rows of organised files and hard drives, velvet pouches sparkling with diamonds, bundles of cash wrapped in plastic, and crates of weapons, all carefully arranged.

Evidence of everything Lucas had built and destroyed.

Leo was staggered. He had prepared himself for something–perhaps a hidden ledger, maybe a stash of incriminating documents. But this? This was beyond anything he had imagined. A treasure trove of secrets, confessions, and deals that revealed the rotten core of Lucas's empire. Leo could hardly breathe as he flicked through the files, his hands trembling with disbelief and a flicker of exhilaration. Lucas wasn't just a crime lord–he was a monster hiding in plain sight. And now, in Leo's hands, lay the power to bring about his downfall.

For a moment, Leo was paralysed by the sheer scale of it. He thought of his mother, Elena, her hands raw from years of labour, her dignity stripped away by poverty and fear. He thought of Liza, her laughter a fragile light in their world, her faith in him unbroken even when he'd lost faith in himself. He thought of all the promises he'd made – to protect, to provide, to be better than the men who had failed them. This was his chance. He could use this evidence to negotiate for safety, bring Lucas to justice, and finally secure a future for his family free from fear.

He moved quickly, gathering files, hard drives, and a few pouches of diamonds into his duffel bag with a sense of urgency. His mind buzzed with endless possibilities. He considered going to the police, but he wondered if he could truly trust them. Lucas had eyes and ears everywhere. He thought about disappearing to start anew, but his thoughts kept returning to Liza. And what about his mother? This wasn't just about himself anymore – he had to see this through for their sake.

He was almost finished when suddenly he heard a soft scuff of a boot on the concrete, which sent a shiver down his spine. Heart pounding, he switched off the flashlight, took a deep breath, and slowly drew his gun, ready for anything.

A shadow moved at the far end of the warehouse. Leo gently pressed himself against a stack of crates, trying to keep his breath steady. The footsteps grew nearer, calm and steady. From the darkness, a tall, broad-shouldered figure appeared, his face hidden in shadows.

"Leo?"

The voice was quiet and familiar: Albert. Lucas's cousin and trusted aide. Once, they had been like brothers, bonded by shared hardship and ambition. Now, they stood on opposite sides of a line that could not be crossed.

Leo's grip on the gun tightened, heart pounding as icy fear coursed through him. He knew he had been discovered, and there was no way to talk his way out of it or escape.

Only survival.

Albert's eyes darted to the duffel bag and the open crates, a flicker of anger crossing his face. His lips curled into a snarl as he barked, "You stupid bastard. You think you can walk away?"

A heartbeat passed, then another.

Albert quickly reached for his weapon.

The first shot rang out, deafening in the confined space. Leo didn't hesitate. He acted on instinct, muscle memory honed in fire. The gun kicked in his hand, the bullet finding its target. Albert staggered, a gurgled curse on his lips before collapsing to the ground.

For a moment, silence prevailed. Then chaos broke out.

Shouts echoed from outside, while footsteps pounded on the concrete.

Leo didn't hesitate for a moment. He sprinted forward, the duffel bag bouncing against his back, adrenaline surging like a fiery tide. He wove through the maze of crates, swiftly ducking behind a stack of tyres as bullets whistled past overhead. Battering through a side door, he stumbled into the night, his lungs burning softly from the exertion.

He sprinted down the alley, vaulting over a chain-link fence and weaving through the maze of the docks. He could hear them behind him—Lucas's men, shouting, searching, and hungry for blood.

He ducked into a narrow alley, pressed himself flat against the wall, and forced himself to breathe. He had known this would be difficult, but now he recognised the truth.

There was no going back.

Lucas would never cease hunting him, not after this. Leo had crossed a line, and the consequences would ripple out, affecting everyone he loved.

But Leo had made his decision, and now he was truly free—free from Lucas's grip, free from the lies and fear that had haunted them for so long. He finally had enough evidence to confront the man who had poisoned their lives for so long and bring him to justice.

But he still had one job remaining.

He quietly reflected on Liza, hearing her voice in his mind ask, "Is this really who you want to be?" His thoughts drifted to his mother, her tired eyes and silent strength reminding him of what truly mattered. He knew he had made terrible choices and done horrible things he could never undo. Still, he felt a flicker of hope—this was his chance to set things right and find a better path.

He slipped into an abandoned shed, his hands trembling as he examined the contents of the bag. Everything was intact—enough to end Lucas's reign, provided he could pass it to the right person.

His phone buzzed—a message from Liza. Just three words: Are you okay?

He wiped the sweat from his brow and took a deep breath, trying to stay focused. He knew he couldn't go home just yet – he had to protect his family from Lucas's men. With determination, he decided he would have to see this through on his own.

He quietly slipped out into the night, moving with a clear purpose. He knew people—those who disliked Lucas just as much as he did—who could help him get the evidence to where it needed to go. He had to trust them; there was no other option.

As he moved through the city's shadows, Leo felt something he hadn't experienced in years—a flicker of hope. Yes, he was being chased and afraid, but he was also truly alive—more alive than ever before. He was determined to hold on to that feeling, whatever the cost.

As dawn unfurled over the city, colouring the sky with hope for a brand-new day, Leo made a heartfelt promise to persevere. It was for Liza, for his mother, and for himself.

He was determined to see through what he had started, and perhaps, just perhaps, he would discover redemption along the way. Yet before redemption, another reckoning awaited him.

Chapter 7
Present Day - The Resort on the Cliff

After five years in the wilderness, Leo Carlos finally reached a charming resort on the outskirts of Goa. But he wasn't the same man who had once roamed the backstreets of Panaji—his bruised knuckles and restless ambition driving him forward. This Leo appeared like a completely different person.

The edges of his former life had been delicately smoothed and shaped by wealth and time. He stepped out of a sleek black luxury saloon, feeling the ocean breeze gently flutter the tailored lines of his charcoal suit. His sunglasses concealed eyes that were sharp and observant, missing nothing. Now, he was a man of influence and power, a complete transformation from the street fighter who had once battled his way through the city's underbelly.

After fading from the world, Leo pieced his life back together, brick by brick. Initially, he operated from the shadows, relying on his street smarts to navigate the complex underworld of business and crime. He mastered the arts of power, negotiation, and control. The days when brute force was his only weapon had passed. Now, he wielded influence like a scalpel, cutting through obstacles with precision.

His first significant opportunity arose in Mumbai, where he made his mark in the shipping industry—an area notorious for corruption and secret dealings. He began cautiously, using his network to ensure some shipments arrived punctually, while others mysteriously disappeared. Over time, he expanded into property, technology investments, and high-stakes trading. His wealth increased swiftly, but so did the number of people who perceived him as a rival.

He thought about how far he'd come. Once, his fists had been his only currency, traded in back alleys and bare-knuckle fights. Now, he walked into boardrooms with the same confidence, sealing deals with a steady hand and an unshakable stare. The tank tops were gone, replaced by tailored suits; the dim bars swapped for exclusive clubs and glittering five-star hotels. At poker tables, he sat across from millionaires, clinked glasses with politicians, and learned to taste the sharp bite of caviar as if it had always been his world. Yet beneath the polished veneer, the same instincts lingered—the raw edge that had kept him alive on the streets. No suit or cigar could strip that away.

The resort was a vision of opulence—a palace of white stone and glass perched on the cliffs overlooking the Arabian Sea. The sun dipped towards the horizon, casting a golden glow over infinity pools and terraces adorned with guests sipping cocktails. It was the sort of place where secrets were whispered behind champagne flutes, and wealth secured more than mere luxury.

Leo walked through the grand entrance, past towering pillars and a chandelier that spilt warm light across the marble floor. He moved with the confidence of a man who belonged, even if he still felt the tug of his past beneath his skin. He was here on legitimate business—business that was above board, yet his instincts warned him that nothing in a place like this was ever straightforward.

And then, he sees her. Maddy Nik.

His heart skips a beat, and in that moment, the years seem to melt away. He is no longer the man hardened by crime and consequences—he is just Leo, standing close to the girl who once lit up his world.

She stood at the bar, her silhouette illuminated by crystal sconces, framed in the elegant satin of her emerald gown. Her beauty had only grown more striking, radiating refined charm and an effortless ability to command a room with a simple tilt of her chin.

Their eyes meet, and in that moment, they exchange a fleeting look of recognition. But then, a shadow of something more—something slightly dangerous—dances in their gaze, hinting at mystery and excitement.

Leo approaches her with deliberate, steady steps. It has been many years since he last saw Maddy, not since that unforgettable night when everything changed forever. She had moved on, while he lingered in the shadows of a world he struggled to understand. Yet, here they are, caught in a place where power and deception drift around them like a faint, tempting scent. He recalled her laughter echoing through narrow alleys, the smell of sea breeze in her hair, and those stolen evenings under starlit skies when love felt everlasting and pure.

The bar was a refuge of wealth and hidden truths, where deals were made through whispered words and meaningful glances. Maddy felt comfortable here. Leo had learned about her history with Raj and was fully aware of her previous escapades. They existed within the same realm. He understood she thrived in environments like this, where the hierarchy was unspoken but clearly understood.

The air is filled with delightful scents of aged whisky and luxurious perfume, blending beautifully with the gentle jazz melodies drifting from a grand piano in the corner.

Leo approaches her cautiously, each step deliberate, wondering if she will recognise him or see him as just another ghost from her past. She experiences a whirlwind of emotions—wanting to slap him yet yearning to embrace him. When he finally reaches the bar, she responds with a subtle smirk, acknowledging him in her own quiet way.

"Leo," she says softly, her voice like silk, gently caressing the skin.

"Maddy."

Their eyes meet, sharing a thousand unspoken words, forging a beautiful bond. For just a moment, it feels as if time pauses, as they are entirely lost in that deep, meaningful gaze. Then, with a gentle breath, they reach out, clasping hands tenderly and embracing warmly, as if afraid the past might slip away between them.

The bartender, sensing the charged atmosphere between them, gently refills her glass with a lovely, deep red merlot. Maddy picks it up, holding the stem gently between her fingers as if pondering the significance of this heartfelt moment.

"I never imagined you would show up somewhere like this."

He smirks. "You say that like it's a compliment."

She chuckles, taking a slow sip of her drink. "It's an observation."

She tilts her head slightly, pondering his words. He has changed. She notices it in how he now carries himself—more guarded, more cautious. The boy she once knew had been raw and reckless. The man before her was completely different, shaped by experience and sharper-edged.

"Are you going to sit?" she asks, gesturing to the barstool beside her.

He hesitates for a moment before gently settling onto the stool, close enough to catch her enchanting perfume—something dark, with lovely hints of jasmine and vanilla. It suits her. He watches as she slowly sips her wine, her fingers calm and steady, showing no sign of the tension that flickers between them.

"How long has it been?" she asks, breaking the silence.

"Five years."

"Five years," she echoes, a wistful note hidden beneath her otherwise steady tone. "A lifetime."

Leo observes her. The dim light emphasises the curve of her cheekbone, and her lips part slightly, as if about to say something she shouldn't. Memories flood back, unbidden, forcing their way to the surface.

Their first meeting took place in humbler surroundings: a shabby club on the outskirts of town, the kind of place where desperation and ambition fed off each other equally. Maddy was a vision even then, standing in the flickering neon light, her eyes filled with something dangerous and intoxicating. He was young, foolish, and completely unprepared for her.

Leo leans slightly forward, resting his forearms on the bar. "What are you doing here, Maddy?"

She traces the rim of her glass with a delicate finger before replying. "The same thing I've always done, Leo. Surviving."

She meets his gaze, and for a moment, the mask falters. A hint of something raw flashes across her face—perhaps regret or something even more profound. Then, just as swiftly, it vanishes, replaced by the carefully constructed façade she wears so skilfully.

"Are you?" he asks, tilting his head. "Surviving?"

She exhales a slow breath. "Barely."

A small, knowing smile curls his lips. "Then we're still the same, after all."

For a moment, they share a quiet connection—an echo of old betrayals and unfinished conversations. But just as they begin to speak, a voice suddenly cuts through the gentle hum of the pub, grabbing their attention.

"Mr. Carlos, your suite is ready."

A friendly attendant stood nearby, looking poised and helpful. Leo smiles and gives a warm nod, glancing at Maddy one last time before he heads away from the bar. "Enjoy your holiday," he says softly.

She smiles, but an inscrutable element lingers in her expression. "Don't get too comfortable, Leo. The past has a way of catching up with you."

He walks away, her words hanging over him like the weight of a storm on the horizon.

—

When the Night Was Theirs: A Prelude to Leo and Maddy

Goa, Seven Years Ago

It was the kind of night that made the streets perspire, thick with humidity and the smell of saltwater and spilled rum. The neon lights of the backstreets near Panaji flickered like dying stars, casting fractured halos over puddles and faded posters of forgotten Bollywood idols. The world here existed in shades of grit and desperation–a place where dreams came to die or be stolen.

Leo knew these streets like the back of his hand. They had shaped him, challenged him, and pushed him to fight for every inch of ground. His calloused knuckles and reputation followed him everywhere, from smoky pubs to underground fights. People were intimidated by him because he never backed down when things got tough.

With nothing to lose, he became a force to be reckoned with.

But that night, fate had a different plan for Leo.

He first spotted her at the Velvet Moon, a run-down little pub hidden away in an alley that reeked of fish guts and spilt petrol. It was the sort of place where the beer was warm, the lights were soft and dim, and the regulars were men with stories they rarely shared happily. She was working behind the battered wooden counter, pouring cheap whisky into chipped glasses, her movements smooth and deliberate. Yet, there was something about her that made her truly stand out amidst all the grime and decay.

She wasn't dressed to impress—cutoff jeans, a faded t-shirt clingy in the heat—but even so, she carried herself with an elegance that didn't belong in a place like this. Her hair was tied in a messy knot, strands sticking to her neck, and her eyes—those wide, dark eyes—were both defiant and exhausted, as if she had been fighting her whole life and still wasn't sure whether the battle was worth it.

Leo watched her quietly from the shadows, nursing a beer, in a spot where no one paid much attention to strangers. It was clear she didn't enjoy being there. You could see it in her avoiding eye contact and in her smile that never quite reached her eyes. She moved as if she were always ready to leave.

Later that night, the trouble started.

Three local thugs—drunk, entitled, the kind of men who believed the world owed them—cornered her behind the bar at closing time. Leo noticed it coming even before the first insult escaped their lips. He recognised the type. He used to run with them.

"Come on, sweetheart," one of them slurred, leaning over the counter. "Why don't you pour us another, eh?"

"We're closed," she said, voice flat but steady. "Get out."

“Don't be like that. We're thirsty, and we've got money.”

Leo noticed the flicker of fear across her face, quickly masked by stubbornness. She was used to dealing with men like this. One of them leaned over the counter and grabbed her wrist.

Leo was on his feet before he realised it.

The first man didn't notice the punch coming at all. Leo eagerly drove his fist into the thug's jaw with a satisfying crack that quickly silenced the pub. The second man reached for a broken bottle, but Leo gently disarmed him with a quick knee to the ribs, causing him to stumble onto a nearby table. The third man paused for just a moment, giving Leo a chance to stare him down, with his blood pumping and his instincts sharper than ever.

"Try it," Leo growled, low and lethal.

They did not.

The thugs slinked away, nursing their bruises and muttering curses under their breath. The pub descended into an uneasy silence, with patrons avoiding Leo's gaze, and no one daring to intervene.

Maddy stood behind the counter, feeling somewhat frozen, her chest rising and falling quickly. Leo turned towards her, half expecting her to reprimand him for stepping in. Instead, she simply gazed at him, her lips parting as if she wanted to share something, but the words seemed to get stuck halfway.

"You alright?" Leo finally asked, his voice rougher than he intended.

She blinked, as if seeing him for the first time. "Yeah. I... Thanks."

He nodded, unsure of what more to say. He had never been good at showing gratitude. He turned to depart.

"Wait," she said, surprising them both.

He paused, glancing over his shoulder.

"Would you like a drink? It's on the house."

Leo chuckled dryly. "After that? Thought you'd throw me out."

She shrugged, a crooked smile tugging at the corner of her lips. "Guess I'm not used to someone... helping."

Leo hesitated before returning and pulling up a stool at the counter. She poured him a glass of whisky—the cheap kind—but it tasted better than anything he had ever known.

He sat silently for a while, the tension easing like worn leather.

"I'm Leo," he said finally.

"Maddy. Maddy Nik"

Their names hung between them, like a fragile bridge over dangerous waters.

That was how it all started.

Over the following months, Leo found himself visiting the Velvet Moon more frequently than he was willing to admit. At first, he justified it as a matter of convenience. The pub was close by, the prices were reasonable, and the shadows provided a comforting hideaway. But deep down, he knew the real reason: Maddy Nik was the cause. There was something about her that made the rough edges of the place seem to fade away.

Maddy was unlike anyone Leo had ever encountered. She had a way of watching the world as if daring it to let her down–again. Sharp, witty in a manner that took him by surprise, and, most importantly, completely unimpressed by his reputation. She didn't flinch when he entered, nor did she hang on to his every word like others did. Instead, she rolled her eyes at his scowls, poked holes in his brooding, and called him out on his nonsense.

"You always look like someone stole your lunch money," she'd tease, sliding him his usual whisky.

"Maybe they did," he replied with his deadpan expression.

That became their thing–banter that softened the jagged edges of their nights. They began to converse: long, relaxed chats over shared cigarettes and cheap drinks, with their laughter blending into the static hum of the broken ceiling fan.

Maddy opened about her childhood, sharing a life profoundly shaped by the sea and a sense of longing. She grew up without a mother, cared for by a gentle, weathered fisherman father who didn't speak much, but whose hands told stories of hardship and resilience. Their small shack sat at the edge of the village, where the waves roared and the wind carried the salty smell of the ocean and old hopes.

From a young age, Maddy learnt to mend nets with calloused fingers and carry baskets heavier than her frame could handle. She knew the names of fish, the moods of the tides, and how to spot a storm before the sky changed. Yet, even as she worked, her eyes were always fixed on the horizon. She would lie awake at night, staring through cracks in the roof, imagining distant cities filled with street music and lights that never went out.

While the other girls dreamed of weddings and feasts, Maddy imagined train tickets, stage lights, and lively cafés in Paris where people wrote poetry on napkins. She longed to dance on cobblestones, sip wine on sunny Greek islands, and become someone who truly mattered–someone the world didn't just glance at, but remembered.

Perhaps I'll open a bookstore in Barcelona," she said once, with a mischievous gleam in her eyes.

Leo chuckled. "You? A bookstore? You don't even read."

"Exactly," she grinned. "That's the trick. I'd only stock books with cool covers."

He recounted his past–the fights, the gangs, the scrappy boy who had to learn to throw punches before he could spell his own name correctly. The constant struggle to survive on the streets that consumed boys like him and spat them out even worse.

They were both broken in various ways. Perhaps that's why they fit.

On quiet nights, they would play cards, with Maddy grinning wickedly when she won. "Face it, Carlos, you're only good at punching people."

"And you're only good at cheating," he'd retort, but with a grin that always reached his eyes when it was her.

They enjoyed midnight snacks from street vendors, debating whether the pav bhaji from Candolim was better than the one from Panaji.

"You have no taste, Carlos. Candolim's is spicier.

"Spicy doesn't mean it's better. That's just how you numb your tongue to forget you're eating rubbish."

"Oh, you're hopeless," she'd laugh, shoving a spoonful of the fiery stuff into his mouth, daring him to say otherwise.

They spent Sundays relaxing on the beach, with Leo attempting (and failing) to teach her how to skip stones.

"It's not skipping if it sinks, genius," she'd mock, folding her arms as his stone plopped into the water like a sulking child.

"It's called a power shot."

She laughed so much that she snorted, and Leo realised at that moment it was the most delightful sound he had ever heard in his life.

They became each other's safe haven. When the outside world felt harsh and overwhelming, they created their own cosy bubble–where debts, threats, and the roughness of the streets could not reach them. During those cherished stolen moments, it was just the two of them, sharing a peaceful retreat.

Leo showed her parts of Goa that no tourist had ever seen–hidden beaches with pristine sand, abandoned forts where they could weave ghost stories, and rooftops where they could lie side by side, gazing at the sky and discussing everything and nothing.

She showed him that life offered more than just survival. She made him laugh and feel valued beyond his fists and street name.

They danced in the rain during the monsoon, their laughter echoing through deserted streets. She tugged him along when he complained about his wet shoes and soaked clothes.

"Come on, grumpy. You'll melt if you stay indoors."

“Maybe I want to melt," he'd grumble, but she was already tugging at his arm, spinning in the pouring rain, her face tilted towards the sky.

They became intoxicated on cheap feni, daring each other to outlandish bets–such as who could hold their breath the longest underwater.

Maddy won, although she claimed that Leo had cheated by nudging her in the face. "You're worse than a sore loser. You're a dirty fighter."

“And you're a cheat with lungs like a bloody whale.”

They came up with some wild ideas–like fleeing to Paris, opening a cosy beach shack that only serves tea and tall stories, or even joining a circus.

"I could be the knife thrower," Leo joked.

Maddy laughed. "You? More like the grumpy clown."

"Clowns wear makeup. That's more your thing."

They teased each other, shared laughs, and stole kisses beneath the shimmering stars as the nights grew silent and inviting. Their love wasn't perfect like a fairy tale–it was wonderfully messy, full of lively moments, sprinkled with sarcasm, playful jabs, and tender stolen kisses in dark alleyways.

She didn’t hold back. “You hide behind your walls, Carlos. Every time things get real, you shut down.”

"You think if you let me see the real you, I'll run? Hello, Carlos. Newsflash! I already see you."

"Yeah?" he'd smirk, masking the lump in his throat. "What do you see?"

She poked his chest. "A stubborn idiot who thinks the only way to survive is alone."

They spent countless nights on that old rooftop, lying on their backs, counting stars and challenging one another to dream bigger.

"I want to see snow," she'd whisper, tracing constellations with her fingers.

"I want to punch someone in the snow," he'd add, and she'd slap his arm, giggling.

They were foolishly in love, clutching at a fragment of happiness they understood the world would not permit them to keep.

And deep down, Leo understood it as well.

Because perfection was never intended to endure in his world.

It all began with quiet whispers. More influential figures started noticing Leo, offering him opportunities that carried both risk and promise–roles that pulled him deeper into Goa's gritty underworld –Panaji. This city seemed to hold everything he ever desired.

He convinced himself he was doing it all for them, dreaming of a brighter future and those whimsical plans for bookstores and beach shacks. Yet, deep down, Leo was changing. He was becoming stronger, a little more guarded, and somewhat darker inside. He was no longer the person who belonged on those rooftops.

Maddy noticed it too.

At first, she would joke about his new jackets, the way he wore them like armour.

"Look at you, Mr. Fancy Pants. What's next? Pinky rings and bodyguards?"

"Don't tempt me."

But beneath the teasing, silences grew deeper over the following months. She would gaze at him longer, as if searching for the boy who used to trip over his own shoelaces at the beach.

He would stay out longer, make excuses, and bring her gifts she never asked for–silk scarves, perfumes, and trinkets from the city. She would smile and thank him, but they both knew it was his way of buying time. Buying distance.

"You can't bribe me, you know," she'd say softly once, her voice almost breaking.

Leo kissed her then, fiercely and desperately, as if the longer he kissed her, the lies between them would fade away.

But they didn't.

The lies kept piling up, just like the phone calls he took in alleyways, the bruises on his knuckles he stopped trying to explain, and the lingering scent of Goa on his clothes.

It happened on a night much like any other. At least, that's how Leo would remember it later. Ordinary. Routine. Until it wasn't.

They sat on their rooftop, the one overlooking the crooked skyline of Panaji, where the stars always seem a little dimmer than they should be. Maddy had brought a bottle of feni, still half full from their last drunken wager, and Leo brought along himself – or at least the version of him that still knows how to sit still.

They didn't talk much that night. The silences between them had grown heavier over the past few weeks, filled with words neither of them dared to voice. Each time Leo tried to speak, the words became tangled in his throat. How does one tell someone that you're slipping into a world they can't follow? That the dreams you shared were slipping further out of reach with every dirty job, every bloodstained promise?

Maddy finally broke the quiet.

"You've been somewhere else lately." Her voice was soft, but it cut deeper than any blade Leo had ever faced. She wasn't accusing him. She never did. It was worse than that. She was... letting him confess.

He gazed at the skyline, watching the flicker of distant lights. It was easier than looking at her. "Maybe I've just been tired."

"Of what?"

"Of this." He gestured vaguely. The city. The streets. The fight that never ended.

But what he really meant was–about pretending.

She smiled with sadness, as if she already knew. Perhaps she always had.

"You know, you can deceive yourself, Leo. But don't deceive me. I'm not a tourist. I've noticed the cracks in you ever since the day you walked into my bar."

He swallowed. His throat was sore. "Maybe I'm already past fixing, Maddy."

She reached out, gently tracing the scar on his cheek with her thumb, as soft as a whisper. "Maybe we're all broken. Doesn't mean you have to break up alone."

He wanted to tell her everything then–how he was leaving, and how tomorrow's job wasn't just a routine task. It was the one–the job–that would take him further away from Goa.

But the words wouldn't come.

Instead, he pressed into her touch, breathing in her scent as if it were his final breath. She carried the smell of rain, of salt, of things he would never hold again.

They kissed. It wasn't like their other kisses–those messy, hungry ones fuelled by feni and foolish dreams. This one was slow and lingering, as if they both knew it was the last.

Maddy was the first to pull away, her forehead resting against his. "Promise me something, Carlos."

"Anything."

"Don't disappear without saying goodbye."

His stomach twisted. He lied. "I won't."

She smiled as if she didn't believe him. Perhaps she didn't need to. Perhaps some goodbyes are louder when they're left unsaid.

They drifted to sleep on that rooftop, side by side, her head resting on his shoulder, his arm around her. For a moment, it almost felt enough. It was as if they were those two children again, intoxicated by love and fanciful dreams.

As the sun rose over the horizon, Leo gently moved away from her comforting warmth. She stirred softly but remained peacefully asleep. Her face looked serene, with her mouth slightly parted and her hair softly tousled by the night breeze, enhancing her tranquil appearance.

He stood there for a moment, observing every tiny detail: her chipped nail varnish, the small scar above her eyebrow, and the faint freckles on her nose that she always tried to conceal.

He yearned to wake her gently, share every small detail, and tell her how deeply he loved her; she was truly the only good thing he'd ever known.

But he chose not to.

Because saying it would make it real. Saying it would make it more complicated.

Then, in that moment, he was gone.

No note. No goodbye.

Maddy woke up to find the Velvet Moon silent, his presence missing. Weeks turned into months, and she heard whispers about a shooting he was linked to. Over the following year, she heard rumours that he had moved to Mumbai, where he began to build a reputation in the lively, bustling city.

She reassured herself with the thought that she hated him for leaving and for not trusting her enough to say goodbye. But the truth was more complex. She genuinely missed him—missed the man who had rescued her, who had made her believe, even if only for a moment, that they might escape the burden of their pasts.

She survived, for that's what Maddy Nik did.

Yet, part of her remained on that rooftop, waiting for a ghost that never came back.

Until now.

Chapter 8
The Meeting at Midnight

Later that evening, Leo settled onto the balcony of his suite, gazing at the waves crashing against the cliffs. The resort's stunning scenery–pristine sands, moonlit waters, and lanterns softly glowing along winding pathways–was beautiful, but appearance isn't everything. For Leo, mastery is what truly matters, and he has dedicated years of hard work and perseverance to achieve it. With determination and careful effort, he has crafted his own world within a realm that once seemed poised to swallow him whole.

Yet, something about this place, about Maddy, seemed like a reckoning.

His phone buzzed as a message came through.

Meet me at the terrace bar at midnight.

No name. But he didn't need one. He knew who it was.

A small flicker of hesitation crossed his mind, a feeling he rarely permitted himself to experience. He had a personal rule to leave the past exactly where it is–buried, forgotten, untouched. Still, Maddy had always been a rare exception.

As midnight struck, Leo wandered through the tranquil resort corridors, feeling the soft scent of salt and jasmine fill the night air. A quiet unease seemed to settle within him, making each step feel a little heavier, as if he was carrying an unspoken burden he couldn't quite see but knew was there.

When he stepped onto the terrace, he discovered a calm, lantern-lit area that was almost empty, with only one figure present, creating a peaceful and intriguing atmosphere.

Maddy leans against the railing, her back turned to him, silhouetted against the dark expanse of water. The sea stretches endlessly before her, turbulent and profound, reflecting something within her that he has never quite understood.

"I didn't think you'd come," she says without turning around.

"I am curious."

She finally faces him, and under the gentle glow of the lanterns, he catches sight of something that makes his heart skip a beat: a hint of hesitation and fear on her face.

That isn't like her at all.

"Leo, you must be cautious," she says softly.

His frown deepens. "What's going on, Maddy?"

She glances around cautiously before stepping closer, her voice soft and pensive. "You might think you've moved on from the past, but it never really lets go of you. There's always someone watching, someone with a reason to want you out of the picture."

A slight chill runs through him from the weight of her words. He's used to being hunted and making enemies, so that wasn't unfamiliar territory. Yet, the way she shares it-with her fingers softly curling around the metal railing as if she were holding herself together—makes this moment feel distinctly different.

More personal and engaging.

"Who?" he asks, maintaining a steady voice.

She hesitates, and in that hesitation, Leo senses something shift—like a ghost of an old wound aching before a storm.

"Your past," she admits, her eyes flickering with something unreadable. "But I have a bad feeling."

Leo scrutinises her, looking for any signs of deception, but all he finds is a hint of something authentic. Something dangerous.

"Where did you hear this?" he asks, slipping back into the sharp, controlled tone that has sustained him for years.

Maddy exhales, crossing her arms. "It doesn't matter. It matters that it's happening."

"It always matters where," he corrects, his voice low. "You don't just appear out of nowhere with vague warnings, Maddy."

She looks away briefly, her fingers softly brushing the delicate silver chain around her neck—an old habit that he remembers well. It is something she used to do whenever she felt nervous, torn between wanting to tell the truth and shielding secrets she wasn't ready to share.

"I heard whispers," she finally says. "People who know people. The kind of people who don't speak unless they have a reason to."

Leo's jaw tightens as he recalls the years he has spent trying to stay ahead of his past. Still, no matter how hard he tries, there is always that one loose end, that one person lurking, waiting for the right moment to strike.

Maddy moves closer, the lantern light flickering in her dark eyes. "I don't know how much time you have before they make their move. But you need to leave."

He lets out a hollow chuckle. "You really think I'm just going to run?"

"I think you're smarter than this," she shoots back. "You have nothing left to prove, Leo. You don't need to stand your ground just because you can."

There is something in her voice—a soft urgency, a hint of something almost desperate—that causes him to pause and listen closely.

"You're scared," he says, noting her reaction.

She doesn't deny it.

"I'm not scared for myself," she murmurs. "I'm scared for you."

Leo feels a change inside, a hint of something that brought back memories he had promised himself he would never face again.

He had been here before, standing at the edge of something with Maddy, her voice softly guiding him towards a place he wasn't quite sure how to reach. It had been years since he allowed himself to think about what they once shared, and what they might have been in another life: a life without bloodshed and betrayal.

But this was not that life.

"Tell me everything you know," he says, voice firm. "Every whisper. Every threat. If I'm being hunted, I need to know who's holding the gun."

Maddy sighs, frustration evident on her face. "You always do this. You never listen."

"I listen," he corrects. "I just don't want to run."

She shakes her head, her gaze searching his. "Then be ready, Leo. Because whoever this is, they're not playing games."

A gentle silence hangs between them, broken only by the calming sound of waves crashing below.

Leo gazes out at the water, the dark expanse stretching endlessly before him. The past is knocking, and this time, it isn't going to let him walk away so easily.

He turns back to Maddy, his expression inscrutable. "Stay close," he says. "And if you hear anything else..."

She concludes, "I'll find you."

He nods, confident that she will.

He tenderly embraces her and walks away, fading into the warm glow of the terrace's twilight. Maddy remains by the railing, her fingers gently holding the chain around her neck, as if lost in thought.

Because there is one thing she hasn't told him.

The things she heard weren't just about Leo; they also involved both of them.

And she is uncertain whether she is warning him in time, or if it is already too late.

Chapter 9
Murder at Midnight

A couple of days pass, and Leo, who is usually a night owl, finds his night taking an unexpected turn. Just as he is about to go to bed, a gentle rustling noise catches his ear. To his surprise, he sees a slip of paper slipped under his door. Curious as ever, he leans down carefully to pick it up, revealing the message bathed in the soft glow of his bedside lamp.

"Meet me in Room 120. Urgent."

His heart pounded as he cautiously approached the door, peering through the peephole with curiosity. The corridor outside looked quiet and deserted, with no footsteps or shadows in the softly lit passageway. It seemed as though whoever left the note had already gone.

Leo hesitates, feeling an uneasy prickle of suspicion. He wasn't expecting any late-night rendezvous—perhaps it's a setup or a plea for help? These questions churn in his mind. Despite his better judgment, he decides to put on his jacket, pick up his keys, and head down the corridor towards Room 120.

When he reaches the room, he notices the door is slightly ajar. Inside, it is pitch dark, with a faint glimmer of moonlight filtering through the curtains. He nudges it open. The scent of whisky and something metallic fills the air. His gaze settles on the figure slumped in the chair.

Even in the almost complete darkness, he can make out a faint glint of light reflecting off a slick stain on the chest—a bullet wound, with crimson blood gradually spreading like ink in water. He sees the head tilted to one side, and the whisky glass nearby, still half-full, its surface catching just enough light to shimmer softly in the shadows.

Leo's breath catches in his throat as a flicker of fear quickly crosses his face, revealing a fleeting moment of vulnerability.

A gun lies nearby as he stands silently, his eyes often drifting to the weapon just a few feet from the lifeless body. A shiver runs down his spine, and as he looks back at the body, a sudden, uneasy twist clenches his stomach.

It's Maddy.

His throat feels desperately dry, and his pulse races, pounding against his skull as if it might burst free. His knees buckle slightly, and he instinctively reaches out for the doorframe for support. A shuddering gasp escapes him as he tries to make sense of the overwhelming sight before him.

Maddy...

Lively, sharp-tongued, and unpredictable, Maddy was the woman who could command a room with just a glance. Now, her body lies lifeless, her signature smirk replaced by a vacant, glassy stare.

No. This can't be happening!

Leo hesitantly takes a shaky step forward, his instincts urging him to act—perhaps check her pulse or call for help? But his mind is torn between this logical course and the overwhelming wave of grief crashing over him, making it impossible to move.

How? How did this happen?

He still recalls the moment just a few hours earlier when they said goodbye after lunch. She appeared to be doing well. They exchanged a few words—though somewhat tense, as always—but nothing indicated what was to come. She had walked away confidently, her head held high, exuding strength.

His chest tightens, and each breath becomes more laborious, making him yearn to wake from this nightmare. The air feels heavy and suffocating, as if the walls are gradually closing in around him. His heart pounds fiercely as he forces himself to take another step forward.

And then he sees it closely.

The gun. His gun.

Leo's mind races as he suddenly realises everything, like a tidal wave crashing over him. The serial number—the weapon he kept hidden—is concealed behind a loose skirting board in his suite. But now, it lies right there, carefully placed beside Maddy's body, like a vital piece of a dark puzzle meant to make him appear guilty.

His hands clench into fists, nails digging into his palms, while his whole body trembles with tension. Panic tightens his throat. His gut warns him he's being set up, trapped in a game where the rules seem stacked against him.

The only certainty he has is that it's his weapon, and even a glance from the police will make him the main suspect.

Someone had intentionally orchestrated this. Every minor detail has been carefully arranged to ensure he is held accountable.

A wave of nausea sweeps over him, causing dizziness and flickering vision. He struggles to keep the bile down, feeling it rise in his throat. He knows he must move—remaining here won't help him escape suspicion.

He takes a closer look at Maddy's lifeless form, a cold weight sinking in his stomach. This isn't just a random murder; it feels like a warning.

But from whom?

His fingers tremble as he reaches for his phone. Calling the police seems like the sensible choice, but the evidence against him is hard to ignore. He can already picture what will happen next: the police will arrive, find the gun, dig into his past, and before he knows it, he will be in handcuffs.

Standing there, frozen, won't help. His instincts scream at him to move, think, and stay one step ahead of whoever set this up.

He takes one last look at Maddy's face, still hauntingly frozen in that eerie, vacant stare, and his jaw clenches tightly. A part of him wants to stay, to try to accept what he is seeing, but there isn't time for that now. Grief is a burden he can't carry.

He is careful not to touch anything unnecessary. Every action is deliberate and cautious. When he gently pushes the door back to how he found it–still slightly open–his fingers softly brush against it. The room must remain looking untouched, just as it is–no signs that anyone has been there after the killer.

Leo feels a tightness in his chest, and just as he was about to look away, something catches his eye–a small strip of black peeking out from beneath the sofa cushion. It is the corner of something smooth and rectangular. He pauses for a moment, uncertain, but then his instincts kick in.

He moves swiftly, crossing the room in two quiet steps and lifting the cushion just enough to catch a glimpse.

A laptop.

His pulse quickens. Whoever did this has overlooked it. Either they were hurried or unaware of its existence. That makes it valuable. Very valuable.

Without a second thought, Leo bends down and picks it up. It feels unexpectedly cold–like it has been lying there for hours. He doesn't pause to see if it will open, nor does he dare switch it on. Slipping it under his jacket, he turns back towards the door, his heart pounding.

He enters the corridor and gently closes the door behind him. The hotel corridor feels alive with unseen presence, amplified by the soft hum of lights and the faint echo of a television in the distance. A surveillance camera in the corner blinks its tiny red light, quietly recording every moment.

Leo walks away with his laptop securely tucked under his arm.

Each step becomes more burdensome than the previous one.

Would they review the footage later and see him?

Would they notice the panic in his stride?

Would it matter if he were innocent?

He turns the corner and quickens his pace. His heart pounds like a thunderous drum in his ears as he rushes back to his suite. His mind is a chaotic tangle, a storm of thoughts colliding with each other.

He needs to think. And breathe.

He reaches his door and fumbles with the keycard. His hands are unsteady, slick with sweat, and it takes him two attempts before the small green light blinks, granting him access. He slips inside and locks the door behind him, leaning against it for a moment as he exhales a tremulous breath.

The silence of the room wraps around him like a suffocating blanket. It now feels strange, different, as if the air itself has shifted.

He drags his hands down his face, trying to steady himself.

His gun, his name, and the crime scene he has been drawn to all seem connected, making the situation feel even more personal and intense.

It all leads to one undeniable conclusion—he has been framed.

But by whom?

His mind races as he paces the room, trying to piece everything together. The invitation—the note slipped under his door. Someone wants him to discover Maddy's body. Not the police, nor the hotel staff. Who?

Why?

Maddy had her fair share of enemies—more than she could easily keep track of. She often played with people like chess pieces, skillfully manoeuvring them to suit her needs. Could it be that she finally crossed the wrong person?

And why involve him in this?

He had kept his distance from her chaos for a long time. Their shared history was complicated, filled with old scars and lingering tensions; still, he made sure to stay away. Deep down, he truly had no reason to wish her harm.

And yet, someone is attempting to suggest that he did.

His eyes flick to the nightstand. He wrenches open the drawer and delves beneath the loose skirting board, his fingers grazing the small, concealed compartment where he hid his gun.

Empty.

His stomach turns.

Someone had been in his room.

Someone had stolen his gun and used it to kill Maddy.

His jaw clenches so tightly it aches.

"Think. Think. Think", he mutters.

His hotel room has a keycard lock. Whoever entered had gained access. A staff member? A professional? Someone who knew exactly where he hid his weapon?

His pulse pounds in his ears.

If they broke into his room, what else might they have taken? Had they planted anything?

He spins on his heel and surveys the room. His duffel bag. His clothes. His laptop is on the desk. He yanks open the wardrobe, his eyes scanning every inch, yet nothing seems out of place. Still, that doesn't mean it hasn't been tampered with.

His breath comes in sharp bursts, and he feels as though he is caught in someone else's game, a puppet being jerked around by unseen strings, evoking a sense of helplessness but also a touch of vulnerability.

Who?

His mind hurriedly considers various possibilities.

Lucas Dada? The crime boss who once saw Leo as a protégé but then they had a falling out? Or was it, Raj? If they wanted revenge, was this his way of serving it cold?

Or someone else altogether?

A couple of hours slip by. A sudden knock on his door startles him.

He freezes.

Did anyone see him leave Room 120? Is it security or the police? His breath catches in his throat. He quickly wipes his palms on his jeans, trying to stay calm and composed.

The knock comes again, more forceful this time.

No choice now.

He takes a deep breath and opens the door.

DIG Aamir, better known as Detective Aamir, looks at him with attentive, friendly eyes, genuinely trying to understand Leo's expression.

"Leo Carlos?"

Leo's throat is dry. He gives a curt nod.

"We need to speak. I am Detective Aamir."

Leo carefully steps aside to let him in, his movements steady and deliberate. Aamir follows closely behind, carrying the quiet confidence of someone who has seen a lot and doesn't easily trust anyone.

The detective asks, "Where were you two hours ago?"

Leo swallows hard. "In my room."

Aamir tilts his head, scrutinising him. "Then why do I have security footage placing you near Room 120?"

Leo feels a heaviness in his heart.

They're already onto him.

"I found a note slipped under my door, and it asked me to go there," he says thoughtfully, carefully choosing his words.

"And did you?"

Leo nods and says, "When I got there, she was dead."

Aamir looks at him with a puzzled expression. "And you left without calling it in?"

Leo clenches his fists. "I'm not stupid. I know how this looks. That gun is mine, but I didn't kill her."

Aamir leans forward. "Then help me understand how your gun ended up at the crime scene."

Leo shakes his head. "Someone broke into my place and stole it. I don't know when."

The detective scrutinises him before exhaling. "For your sake, I hope you're telling the truth."

A knock on the door interrupts their conversation.

A uniformed officer stands outside, holding an evidence bag containing a hotel keycard.

"Found this in the victim's pocket, sir," the officer says, handing it to Aamir.

Leo's stomach clenches as he catches sight of the embossed number–his room number.

"Looks like Maddy paid you a visit before she died," says Aamir. "Care to explain that?"

Leo clenches his teeth.

He is being pulled further into the quicksand.

"I didn't see her," he says.

Aamir still isn't entirely convinced. "Leo, then how did your room key land in her room? If you're innocent, you'd better start proving it quickly!"

Leo realises he has no option.

He must catch the real murderer before the noose tightens around him.

Just as Aamir is about to leave, he pauses briefly and gives Leo a sharp, cautious look.

"Do you know Raj Gambhir?"

A jolt like lightning shoots through Leo's mind. His body tenses, and for a brief moment, he forgets to breathe.

Chapter 10
Past and Present Collide

Raj Gambhir: The Phantom King of Goa's Underworld

Raj Gambhir was more than just a businessman; he was a shadowy figure quietly operating within influential circles, subtly shaping events behind the scenes. His wealth and influence weren't simply handed to him; they were built carefully on blood, betrayal, and crime. He was a cunning manipulator, orchestrating chaos with calm confidence, always staying just out of reach. Officially, he owned a successful chain of shipping companies and was highly regarded among Goa's elite. Yet, unofficially, he was the trusted partner working alongside Lucas Dada, the recognised kingpin of the coastal underworld.

Raj's operations extended well beyond legal activities, constructing a vast empire that concealed a network of illegal dealings. He held significant sway over Goa's ports—everything was conducted solely with his knowledge and approval. Drugs, gold, and stolen art moved effortlessly along his shipping routes. His network appeared unstoppable, with corrupt officials routinely managing customs.

Raj's connections to the political elite were vast. He financed election campaigns, quietly supported struggling politicians, and ensured those in power remained dependent on him. He understood the unwritten rules of the game–money spoke, and in Goa's political scene, it shouted.

Many officials secured their roles through his influence, either by direct support or by subtly sidelining rivals. He ensured that key positions–such as customs officers, port authorities, and select judiciary members–were held by people indebted to him. When issues arose, a swift and discreet phone call was often all that was needed to resolve matters smoothly and quietly.

His influence extended far beyond local politics. Raj had established strong ties with syndicates involved in real estate, film financing, and offshore accounts. He acted as the link between politicians looking to launder money and criminal networks eager to invest in legitimate businesses.

Unlike Lucas Dada, who ruled through fear, Raj blurred the lines between crime and legitimate business so seamlessly that few could tell where one ended and the other began. He funded luxury hotels, high-end casinos, and private clubs, transforming them into centres for money laundering. Wealthy tourists and foreign investors mingled at his venues, unaware that they were on the ground where backdoor deals were struck, fortunes built, and threats whispered in hushed tones over expensive whisky.

His charisma made him a favourite among industrialists and celebrities, who turned a blind eye to his criminal dealings in exchange for protection and connections. He was often seen at elite gatherings, shaking hands with top businessmen, some of whom had skeletons in their closets that only Raj knew of. He provided them with security and ensured their illegal activities remained well concealed, and in return, he expanded his network of power and influence.

Raj had built a thriving empire hidden within Goa's lively tourism scene. Raj's name was whispered in corridors where rules were often bent, in meeting rooms where deals were struck, and on the streets where fear persisted.

He had the uncanny ability to turn problems into opportunities, becoming the unseen force that dictated the pace of Goa's underworld. And as long as he kept those in power in his pocket, he remained untouchable.

Lucas recognised that every king benefits from having a trusted partner – a clever strategist, a diplomat, someone capable of navigating the subtleties of leadership with grace and tact in high society. Raj was that person for him. If Lucas was the sword, Raj was the scalpel. He ensured everything ran smoothly, forged valuable alliances, and faced challenges with quiet skill and ease, making a real difference behind the scenes.

Unlike Lucas, who thrived on overt displays of power, Raj played the long game. While Lucas held the reins of power through brute force, Raj ensured the machine continued to run, making himself indispensable to the empire.

When rival gangs attempted to encroach on their territory, Raj orchestrated discreet assassinations that left no trace. When an ambitious customs officer refused to turn a blind eye to a substantial drug shipment, it was Raj who ensured the man suddenly found himself embroiled in a fabricated corruption scandal, destroying his career and life. Raj's power stemmed from the fact that he never needed to raise his voice—his enemies simply understood that to defy him meant their destruction.

Their Smuggling Empire

Lucas controlled the underworld, while Raj was the brains behind its most profitable operation—smuggling. Gold, drugs, weapons, and even stolen luxury goods moved seamlessly through their network, all hidden by Goa's thriving tourism and commerce.

Tourist traffic provided them with natural cover, making their activities less noticeable. Cargo ships disguised as fishing vessels transported weapons and heroin, while luxury yachts carried synthetic drugs for wealthy clients. Even unsuspecting foreign backpackers often became unwitting mules, with their luggage secretly filled with diamonds or powdered narcotics. What made Raj's system truly clever was its duality: each illicit activity was carefully concealed behind a seemingly legitimate facade.

He had an exceptional talent for transforming liabilities into opportunities. Old warehouses near the Vasco docks were converted into lively seafood processing centres and attractive boutique wineries. Some even became busy import-export hubs trading exotic spices and handcrafted artefacts. Although these businesses appeared legitimate, they often concealed a darker reality—fish crates with false bottoms filled with cocaine, wine barrels sealed with micro-diamonds in waterproof capsules, and European liquor shipments secretly transporting contraband in hidden compartments.

Customs rarely scrutinised matters closely, and Raj made sure it stayed that way. Using a network of bribes, threats, and calculated blackmail, the ports became his domain. Officers turned a blind eye, shipping manifests were altered, and even the occasional inspection was carefully staged beforehand. High-level connections within customs and the local police ensured smooth passage. If a junior officer grew too curious, he was transferred. If a journalist began investigating, they were either silenced or paid off.

At the centre of everything was Raj's tidy and inviting office, nestled within a modest seafood export facility on the outskirts of Panaji. The walls were decorated with simple, tasteful artwork. A beautiful teak desk offered a lovely view of the Mandovi River. Nearby, a black-and-white photograph of a young Raj sat beside a framed quote: "Control the tide, not the boat."

It was fascinating how, even though everyone was aware of the situation, no one dared to take action. Those brave enough to confront him often found themselves either harmed, disappeared, or unexpectedly drawn into his world. The docks, much like Raj's chessboard, saw every move dictated by him. While Goa might appear to outsiders as a paradise, for Raj it was the perfect setting for building his secret empire.

Even Lucas Dada, despite his great power and presence, could not overlook how Raj transformed crime into commerce, establishing a kingdom of secrets in Goa.

One of Raj's most ingenious schemes involved the cruise ships that docked at Goa's ports. These luxury vessels brought in thousands of tourists each month, many of whom unknowingly aided his smuggling operations. Select guests received lavish gift bags–perfumes, jewellery, handbags–all with hidden compartments. Unaware, they carried contraband across international borders. By the time customs officials caught on, the goods had already vanished into the black market.

Raj's empire stretched far beyond Goa, supported by a tightly organised network of intermediaries. Each person had a specific role, ensuring loyalty and strict secrecy. Ambition or rebellion came at a high cost–some disappeared entirely, erased from all records. Others washed ashore in Goa, lifeless; their fate served as a grim warning that betrayal could be deadly. Fear, rather than loyalty, maintained his empire.

Raj's trusted aide Vikram handled the logistics with great care and attention. With his background as a marine engineer, Vikram possessed a wealth of knowledge in modifying cargo containers to evade detection by X-ray scans and sniffer dogs. Thanks to his skill, shipments went smoothly, often arriving at ports during quieter hours to avoid detection. He also coordinated the dispatch of several decoy shipments in advance, effectively keeping customs officials guessing and protecting the real cargo from scrutiny.

Despite his brilliance, Raj was a man full of contradictions. On one hand, he was regarded as a generous philanthropist–the type of businessman who seemed to have a golden touch. On the other hand, those on the outside sometimes saw him as a brutal kingpin, willing to do whatever it took to defend his empire. Raj could display warmth and friendliness during a game of chess, yet he would also be plotting strategies that might turn violent. He understood that true power wasn't just about instilling fear but about being an integral part of everything. His rivals often misunderstood him, sometimes believing his charm was a sign of weakness. For him, every move was carefully and thoughtfully planned to guarantee success.

Raj harboured ambitious dreams of growth. He saw himself not just as the mastermind behind the smuggling empire but also as its clear leader. He began forming discreet partnerships, establishing connections with South American cartels, Russian arms dealers, and even former intelligence operatives skilled in counter-surveillance. With detailed planning, he was working towards a significant new venture that could truly reshape the power landscape forever.

The only person Raj ever genuinely feared was Lucas Dada. The old crime boss was incredibly clever and resourceful, having weathered numerous betrayals and intense power struggles. Raj understood that, despite his own brilliance, he was still navigating within Lucas's territory. Even the tiniest hint of disloyalty or ambition beyond what was permitted could put Raj at serious risk of falling from grace.

A Partnership Built on Mutual Gain

Lucas may have controlled Goa's underworld, but Raj was the real reason it remained untouchable. Their partnership was built on mutual reliance–Lucas provided the muscle, while Raj supplied the brains. While Lucas surrounded himself with enforcers, Raj moved with lawyers, accountants, and politicians who kept their empire secure. Their bond wasn't just about friendship, but about the powerful truth that, together, they were unstoppable.

They were far from ordinary criminals; they were masterminds shaping a world where crime flourished unchecked. As new rivals emerged and politicians grew more unpredictable, even the police sometimes struggled to resist their sway. Yet Raj always devised a clever escape plan–if bribes failed, blackmail followed; if blackmail was thwarted, fatal "accidents" often occurred. In their world, one rule was paramount: play the game and prosper or vanish without a trace.

They had often faced difficulties maintaining control over Goa's criminal activities. One of the biggest challenges came from a rising politician, Devender Joshi, whose influence posed a notable threat.

Joshi built a strong reputation as a passionate defender against corruption. Unlike many politicians who accepted bribes and overlooked wrongdoings, he sincerely dedicated himself to cleaning up Goa's underworld. He carried out numerous investigations into smuggling routes, targeted corrupt officials, and even openly named Lucas Dada and Raj Gambhir as the masterminds behind the state's organised crime network. His speeches were heartfelt, and his determination stayed unwavering. He gained widespread support from the people, who saw him as a symbol of hope in a system often clouded by corruption. The media lauded him as the individual who might finally bring justice to Goa's underworld.

For the first time in years, Raj sensed a genuine threat to their empire. Lucas, as usual, was eager to retaliate against Joshi–whether through an assassination, a car bomb, or some other dramatic and visible method. However, Raj understood that such direct actions might draw too much attention, and that was the last thing they wanted. Instead, he carefully devised a more subtle and clever plan.

Raj carefully orchestrated a scandal. His team skilfully planted evidence to connect Joshi to an offshore account filled with laundered money. Meanwhile, a false witness–someone Raj had prepared for this moment–stepped forward, claiming that Joshi had taken bribes from rival smuggling syndicates. The media quickly picked up the story, and the buzz was overwhelming.

Political analysts discussed whether Joshi might have become entangled in the very web of corruption he had vowed to combat. His supporters were somewhat divided. Some remained loyal, while others hesitated. Small doubts began to emerge.

But Joshi didn't behave like the others. He fought back. Despite his reputation being attacked, he kept pushing for their arrest, threatening to reveal their entire operation. He appeared on national television, denouncing the fabricated charges and exposing the hidden hands that had orchestrated his downfall. He vowed to bring Raj and Lucas to justice, whatever it took. His allies in law enforcement worked even harder, conducting raids, interrogating suspected smugglers, and tightening security at ports.

That was when Raj knew they had no choice.

One rainy evening, Joshi's car skidded off a cliffside road. The official report described it as an unfortunate accident—faulty brakes, a wet road, and a tragic yet common mishap. Yet, those familiar with Raj's ways knew better. A mechanic on Joshi's security team, whose family Raj had kindly supported over the years, had made a simple modification, ensuring the brakes would fail at just the right moment. It was a sleek and clever setup, with no evidence of any foul play.

The media mourned Joshi's passing, feeling it was a significant loss in the fight against corruption. Supporters gathered for candlelit vigils, and protests erupted across the state, expressing their support. Yet, without solid evidence of wrongdoing, the initial surge of outrage eased, causing the investigation to slow down. His successor in office became noticeably more cooperative, understanding that it was wiser to work with Lucas than to face the grave consequences of opposition.

It had been a narrow escape, but their empire remained unharmed. He knew another Joshi could rise someday, another crusader who believed they could overthrow them. The game never ended. It only evolved. And Raj was always prepared to play.

Chapter 11
A Relationship Built on Power and Control

Maddy had always found power fascinating–it wasn't just about appearances, but the intense, vibrant energy that flowed beneath the surface. She was drawn to men in boardrooms, men in uniforms, those who could make things disappear with a simple nod–these were the types she admired most. Raj Gambhir seemed to fit that mould perfectly; however, there had been something about him that made her feel uneasy right from the beginning.

After Leo left her life, Maddy was left with shattered dreams and an insatiable desire for more. She had no home, no family, and no one to rely on. Yet her ambition remained fierce and unwavering. She refused to fade into obscurity. Deep down, she yearned for wealth, fame, and a life far beyond the gutters she had grown up in. She eagerly pursued opportunities, even if it meant risks and sacrifices. This relentless drive eventually led her to Raj. He promised her everything she desired, and although she knew it wouldn't come without a cost, Maddy was prepared to pay it.

Their relationship began as a delicate interplay of seduction and ambition–her gateway into the world of film. Maddy wasn't some naive ingénue; she'd weathered Bollywood's storms without ever truly fitting in. She rose from B-grade thrillers to eye-catching item numbers in commercial hits, and finally to art-house films that lured critics and financiers with hidden agendas. Fame drew her into circles of politicians and smugglers—men craving the allure of a woman both captivating and expendable. Yet Raj was unlike the rest. With him, it wasn't merely about appearances or possession; there was something deeper, something neither of them could ignore.

They met at a luxurious floating casino on the Mandovi River, a lively place where roulette wheels spun as swiftly as the rumours, and fortunes shifted with secret whispers. Maddy was the guest of honour for the evening—stunning, sharp, and already crooking admiration around her. She wore a gorgeous red silk gown that alluded to mystery and carried herself with the grace of someone who had weathered the storm and transformed her experiences into a captivating performance.

Raj did not glance at her as others did. His eyes showed no hunger, no eagerness to conquer or claim. Instead, he watched her like a thoughtful chess player, analysing not just the next move but the fifth, showing calm, deliberate patience.

That intrigued her. Most men desired her. Raj made her desire *him*.

At first, everything seemed quite familiar—gifts, attention, and whispered invitations to his villa in Dona Paula. The diamonds sparkled beautifully, the champagne was perfectly aged, and the silks felt wonderfully luxurious. But what truly drew her in wasn't just the glamour; it was the access it offered. Raj was opening doors to worlds she hadn't even imagined before. He guided her into circles of power–introducing her to ministers at fundraisers, judges at private screenings, and foreign investors aboard luxury yachts.

Maddy was more than just there to entertain; she was quietly absorbing everything around her. She developed beyond merely being a companion–she became a valuable tool. And Raj, always the clever strategist, used her with skill and care.

But beneath the polished façade, their relationship was far darker. Raj didn't shout or raise a hand – he didn't need to. His control was entirely psychological. Every gesture of affection was tinged with a quiet threat. He kept her close, not just to adore her but also to watch her. Maddy, always the manipulator, realised too late that she was the one being manipulated.

She felt lonely. Her friends avoided her. Her movements were subtly monitored by drivers who never left her side, by household staff who reported to someone else. The beachfront villa she once flaunted had been transformed into a gilded cage. When she tried to pull away, the repercussions came swiftly. A leaked video here, a cancelled contract there. An old scandal resurfaced on social media. Her worth was now tied to Raj's interest, and Raj never relinquished easily.

Still, something within her wouldn't break. Perhaps it was pride; maybe it was a survival instinct, but Maddy began to seek a way out. She gathered fragments of secrets, recorded conversations, and memorised names. She recognised that Raj's weakness lay not in his fists or his empire; it was in his arrogance.

And one day, when the moment arrived, Maddy vowed she would not simply walk away.

She would burn the entire stage to the ground.

The Honey Trap

Over the past four years, Maddy wasn't just Raj Gambhir's glamorous companion; she was his most valuable asset. She was like a captivating siren in silk, handling everything with elegance. Raj never had to get his hands dirty when Maddy was around, as she could disarm men with just a glance and win them over with her charming smile.

He used her much like a skilled hunter uses bait, placed carefully, never rushed. She didn't just attract; she observed. She knew exactly how to become what a man desired. For the politicians who believed they could resist Raj's growing influence, she was the challenge, the signal, the trap.

Initially, they were idealistic men, some were pure-hearted, while others lacked experience. They genuinely believed they could challenge Raj's smuggling empire and oppose his control over Goa's ports, casinos, and real estate. They thought their principles gave them strength and influence.

Then Maddy would arrive.

She attended fundraisers, private parties, and yacht galas with a subtle charm. She knew when to flirt, exchanging lingering eye contact and sharing the perfect laugh at the right jokes. A gentle touch on an arm at the right moment added to her allure. She never rushed things, making sure Raj felt that her interest was genuine and worth the wait. Like a trap carefully set, caught at just the right time.

And once the prey believed they were in control, she would lower her guard just enough to make them drop theirs.

Drinks would flow, private invitations would be sent out, and hotel suites would be reserved.

Then came the cameras–hidden behind mirrors, concealed in lamps, disguised within air vents. Raj's men would watch silently, recording every compromising moment. When the footage surfaced - always discreetly, always with a polite warning. It was already too late.

Some men paid; others folded. The utterly foolish ones tried to resist. They disappeared.

Maddy was fully aware of what she was doing. She understood her role in Raj's world of influence and deception. But given her circumstances, what options did she genuinely have?

She had seen what became of those who defied him, witnessed men stripped of power, wealth, and dignity. She had watched one man, a former Corporator, weeping on his knees in Raj's private cellar, pleading for his family's safety before being thrown into a shipping container and vanishing without a trace.

She understood the rules well. As soon as she was no longer helpful, she would face the same outcome.

Thus, her purpose was complete: exquisite, lethal, and utterly irreplaceable.

—

A Cage Made of Gold

Raj never let her forget who she was and, more importantly, who she wasn't.

He subtly reminded her that everything she owned belonged to him. The ocean-view house in Miramar? His name was on the title. The sapphire necklace she wore at the premieres. Gifted, not earned. The luxury cars, the couture gowns, and the guest appearances in high-profile films were obtained through Raj's influence.

"Without me," he would say with a wry smile, "you'd still be sitting at that bar, pouring cheap whisky for drunks. Just another pretty face lost in the crowd, forgotten by midnight. I gave you a way out—a chance to be someone they'd never dare forget."

Initially, Maddy told herself she was biding her time, that she was using him, not the other way around. After all, she had risen from obscurity to stardom. She now possessed influence and power of her own—did she not?

But gradually and quietly, Raj shattered her illusions. She was not a queen; she was a cherished possession, a doll in a designer cage.

She yearned for freedom. The first time she attempted to escape, she didn't even manage to leave the city.

She packed her suitcase, booked a flight to Singapore under a false name, and contacted an old friend in the film industry using a burner phone, all seemed to be going smoothly. However, when she arrived at the airport, she found her ticket had been cancelled and her passport marked. Suddenly, two men in black shirts began following her back to her car, adding to the tension of the moment.

When she returned home, Raj was already there, looking calm and content, smiling softly as he gently swirled his glass of whisky.

"Leave?" he said, as though the idea amused him. "Where would you go, Maddy? Who would protect you?"

She had no answer, trembling and fearing the worst.

The men she had seduced, blackmailed, and betrayed would never offer her refuge. The politicians she had brought to their knees would rather see her gone than risk exposure.

There was no safety. No redemption. Just the cage.

A cage of silk sheets and ocean views. Evenings filled with wine and hollow laughter created a prison built of possessions and wealth, where silence comes at the cost of survival.

And so, she remained. Day after day, smile after smile, lie after lie.

But inside, Maddy was already starting to unravel. Every time she used the honey trap, she felt a little of herself slip away. Even though Raj still showed her off like a trophy, she could see it in his eyes, the way he looked past her now, counting down the days until her worth would fade.

She was already living on borrowed time.

And somewhere in the shadows of her mind, the question echoed like a silent scream: How does one escape a man who owns everything, including you?

The Betrayal That Sealed Her Fate

For years, Maddy had flawlessly fulfilled her role as Raj's ever-smiling companion, masking the venom behind her eyes with captivating charm. She quickly understood that power was currency in Raj's world, and charm was her most effective weapon. She subtly whispered into the right ears, pushed deals ahead, and stroked egos in velvet-lit rooms where decisions were made amid cigars and bloodstained contracts.

To the outside world, she seemed his muse. To the men who feared him, she appeared as wildfire. But Maddy knew better. She was a pawn in disguise as a queen, dancing within a gilded cage.

As time passed, she increasingly felt confined. Raj's influence, though charming on the surface, felt quite restrictive. Every decision she made - every step, word, and outfit–seemed carefully aligned with his aims. While he sometimes showed affection, it often carried a possessive tone. Trust, it appeared, came with its own expectations, and when his anger emerged, it was quiet and unsettling, leaving a profound impression.

She attempted to escape once. She was hesitant to try again.

But even a caged bird dreams of flying.

Then came the offer.

Another syndicate. Fresh money from the north gradually infiltrates Goa's underworld. They had been observing her carefully and noticed the vulnerabilities in Raj's defences reflected in her eyes. One evening, a well-dressed man in a crisp linen shirt quietly slips into the seat beside her at a charity gala. He doesn't need to say much; the message is all there.

"We can get you out."

Money. Protection. A passport with a new name and a one-way ticket to Lisbon. All she needed was to give them something. Anything. Just to harm Raj. Just something, only, she possessed.

Maddy didn't agree immediately, but the offer lingered in her mind, tempting enough to make her reconsider.

She spent nights pacing her bedroom, gazing at her reflection and contemplating her choices as fear churned in her stomach. She remembered the time Raj smiled at a man across the dinner table, only for him to be killed before dessert. She truly understood what he was capable of. Still, in moments of desperation, people can act quite unpredictably.

So, she did it.

A shipment schedule, a name, a time – the kind of information that could dismantle a branch of Raj's network in a swift, bloody blow.

It was supposed to be clean. Quiet. Untraceable. Raj was not meant to find out.

But Raj *always* knew.

When she returned home that night, the lights were off. The room was eerily quiet. The air faintly smelled of sandalwood and danger.

Raj sat in the dark, sipping his whisky, a calm smile on his lips.

"Tell me, Maddy," he said, his voice as smooth as silk, "do you believe in second chances?"

Her heart pounded.

Raj's Revenge

Over the next few days, Maddy noticed the subtle changes. The slight tightening of his jaw and the colder tone when he mentioned her name, yet Raj continued to maintain his outward façade. He still took her to glamorous parties, still placed diamond bracelets on her wrists, and still whispered promises into her ear, acting as if she were the most important person in his life. He played the caring king, and she, the cherished queen.

But the mask he wore was not for her; it was for control.

Maddy reassured herself that it was just paranoia. She had been on edge for weeks. Every phone call startled her, and each knock at the door felt like a warning. Still, she hoped her acts of betrayal remained hidden. She had been cautious–using encrypted apps, disposable phones, and holding secret meetings away from Raj's view.

She underestimated him.

Then one evening, everything changed.

They were at his private villa, perched on the cliffs of Dona Paula, where the sea seemed endless and the sky always glowed gold at sunset. The villa was quiet, almost reverent in its stillness. Maddy was barefoot on the marble patio, sipping a glass of Merlot, finally allowing herself to breathe.

Raj sat opposite her in a low chair, his white linen shirt immaculate, his expression unreadable. The ocean breeze tousled his hair, yet he remained completely still. He watched her with the unsettling patience of a man already aware of the game's outcome.

"You thought you could betray me, Maddy?" His voice was soft, almost amused.

Maddy froze, her glass halfway to her lips. The words sank slowly, like a knife turning in her gut.

"After everything I've done for you?"

Her throat felt tight, and her fingers quivered.

She tried to respond, deflect, and deny – but before should for the lie, he reached into a leather satchel beside his chair and gently slid a thick folder across the table.

She opened it with trembling hands.

Photographs. Crisp, damning.

There she was, getting into a car with one of the northern gang's lieutenants. Another shot of her in a dark alley, swapping a flash drive for a wrapped bundle. Then the screenshots. Her private chats exposed, each message like a dagger: shipment routes, transaction details, whispered promises of escape.

Her breath caught in her throat when she saw the copy of the bank transfer. The timestamp.

But the final image made her stomach turn.

It was her. In a hotel bed. Tangled in sheets. Smiling.

With *Leo from the past.*

Her lover. Her mistake.

The silence between them thickened.

Raj relaxed in his chair, gently swirling his drink as the ice softly clinked, like a gentle heartbeat marking the moment. His eyes, deep and mysterious, remained steadily on hers.

"You disappoint me," he said at last, his tone free of anger, which somehow made it even worse. "I gave you everything. Protection. Power. A seat at the table."

He raised his glass, giving a cool, indifferent toast to the air. "And still, you sold me out."

Maddy was speechless, feeling as though there was nothing left to say. No lies could conceal what was true, and no seduction appeared able to save her now.

For the first time in years, she experienced a real sense of fear—a deep, creeping dread that settles into your bones and softly whispers: This is how it ends.

She had spent years weaving her web of manipulation, pitting men against one another like pieces on a chessboard. But now, in Raj's shadow, she realised the truth—she wasn't the spider.

She was the fly.

Raj finished his drink and rose with a gentle, thoughtful motion.

"I'm not going to kill you," he said, adjusting his cufflinks. "That would be too merciful."

His smile was narrow and final.

"No, Maddy. I'm going to let you live long enough to watch everything you love to disappear."

And just like that, he stepped inside, leaving her alone with the sea—and the sound of the waves crashing like a slow and cruel sentence.

Maddy didn't die that night.

Raj wasn't impulsive like Lucas. He didn't believe in shooting someone in the head or using knives in the dark. That wasn't his style. He preferred patience and precision.

He liked to let betrayal fester, enjoying the sight of his enemies unravelling, thread by thread, until they destroyed themselves trying to escape his shadow.

So, he let her live.

To the outside world, everything appeared unchanged. Maddy continued to attend events in stunning couture, smiling for the cameras alongside Raj, and navigating the glamorous corridors of Goa's elite. However, an unmistakable warmth had vanished. A cold detachment now replaced the gentle gestures, private exchanges, and tender possessiveness. A look of quiet calculation cast a shadow over her steps, as if she were already a ghost softly walking through her final days.

She first noticed the silence. The people who used to call her no longer did, which made her feel quite unsettled. Her usual driver had been replaced by someone new, adding to her growing unease. She realised her phone had been tapped and her passwords had been altered without her knowledge. Then, she received a worrying message from her bank: her account had been frozen.

Piece by piece, her life was being dismantled.

Maddy knew what that meant.

She had become a liability. In Raj Gambhir's world, liabilities did not last long.

She barely slept, feeling anxious with every knock at the door that made her heart race, and every whisper in the hallway that sounded almost like a farewell. Raj didn't need to get his own hands dirty; he had many loyal men who obeyed him out of fear, money, or blood. She wouldn't see it coming, which was precisely how Raj liked to operate.

She longed for a brief escape, a place where she could breathe freely, far from the constant worry of Raj.

She headed to the one place she felt could provide safety. The resort, a stunning seaside retreat, a fortress nestled into the cliffs and far from Raj's usual circles.

Chapter 12
The Past Catches Up

Leo was lost in thought about the detective's question. "Did you know Raj Gambhir?"

If there's one thing that truly sparked the fierce conflict between Raj and Leo, it was Liza Carlos.

Leo had spent his life battling both in the ring and beyond. Yet, nothing had ever pushed him to the brink like this. Nothing had ever made him pull the trigger without hesitation, regret, or second thoughts–until the night Dev Gambhir tried to destroy Liza.

Liza had been the sole bright, unspoiled light in his life–his younger sister, his kin, his only family. She had dreams, a fire burning within her, and a future very different from the violence that had shaped his world. Leo had spent his whole life protecting her, keeping her away from the dirt that came with his fists, from the underworld, and from the men who lurked in the shadows of Goa's elite.

But he had failed.

Liza had never quite found her place in their world. Growing up on the same streets as Leo, she watched as his life was filled with bloodshed and violence. However, she yearned for something different, something beyond the fights, beyond the crime, and beyond the harsh cycle that seemed to imprison men like him. She dreamt of a life outside of Goa, a future with a career and true independence.

That fateful night, after much pestering, Liza reluctantly agreed to help her friend at a party in a luxurious coastal villa. With a couple of volunteers dropping out at the last minute, she had little room to refuse. Resigned, she found herself behind the bar, pouring drinks and trying to blend into the background—yet it was there, in that moment of quiet unwillingness, that she caught the unwavering gaze of Dev Gambhir.

Dev Gambhir was quite different from his older brother, Raj, who was a formidable and respected crime lord known for moving silently through Goa's underground world. Raj was cautious, strategic, and untouchable. In contrast, Dev was impulsive, spoiled, and entirely out of control. Having grown up under Raj's influence, he felt untouchable by law enforcement and revelled in the privileges his name conferred.

The party was bustling with the usual lively crowd—successful businessmen, politicians, shady characters, along with their women. The music filled the villa with energy, drinks continued to flow, and hushed conversations about deals took place behind closed doors. Liza hadn't wanted to come, but her friend had convinced her, assuring her of an evening filled with fun, sophistication, and sights she'd never seen.

She spotted Dev watching her from across the room, his gaze lingering too long and his smirk predatory. She ignored him, dismissing his advances with courteous indifference.

But Dev wasn't used to being ignored.

As the party gradually wound down, cheerful music blended into soft murmurs, while the gentle clinking of glasses created a warm, cosy atmosphere. Liza quietly slipped away from the dwindling laughter, craving a quiet moment just for herself. She wandered into a comfy side room upstairs—a peaceful study filled with old books and inviting dark wood accents. All she needed was her bag; nothing more. She longed to step outside for a breath of fresh air, seeking just a little escape to find some relief. As she reached down to grab it from the drawer, the door creaked gently and closed softly behind her.

Dev was standing there.

He gently leaned against the door, partly shrouded in shadow, carrying the aroma of expensive Scotch. His shirt was slightly unbuttoned, and his smile, though charming, felt a little strange, making Liza feel somewhat uneasy. He seemed a bit tipsy, speaking with a slur, and something menacing lingered beneath his relaxed demeanour.

"You've been running from me all night," he drawled, staggering a step forward, his eyes glinting with hunger and clouded with desire.

"I don't want trouble, Dev," Liza said, her voice steady but her pulse racing like a trapped bird's.

"But trouble," he whispered, circling the room like a predator, "wants *you*."

She instinctively stepped back, clutching her bag to her chest. Before she could scream, he lunged forward. His fingers clamped around her wrist like a vice, yanking her towards him. She struggled and managed to break free briefly, but he caught her again—more roughly this time—pushing her against the edge of the desk. The bag hit the floor. Her breath caught in her throat.

"Let go of me!" she cried, twisting, clawing at his face.

But Dev was stronger—too strong. He overpowered her, pinning her arms above her head as she struggled beneath him, her cries muffled by his weight. His body pressed hard against hers, trapping her. One hand clawed at her waist, fingers digging in, while the other held her down with brutal force. Then, without warning, he forced his mouth onto hers, kissing her with violent hunger, ignoring her pleas and resistance. It was an assault—cruel, calculated, and terrifying.

She sank her teeth into his shoulder, biting down hard and tasting blood. Dev let out a sharp, guttural curse, jerking back in pain.

At that moment, a surge of desperation and fear ignited a strong instinct within her. Her hand moved across the desk, feeling around until her fingers made contact with the solid base of a shiny brass lamp. Without hesitation, she swung it with all her might, driven by a determined impulse.

The lamp cracked against his temple with a sickening thud.

Dev screamed and staggered back, stunned. Liza didn't hesitate.

She ran.

Her heels clicked rapidly on the floor as she hurried down the corridor, tears blurring her sight. Her dress was torn at the back, with a strap hanging loosely. Her hair was dishevelled, and her body trembled with shock and anger. She didn't know if he was behind her, so she didn't stop to look back.

She ran down the stairs, noticing the curious glances and the busy party scene around her, though many seemed too absorbed in their own worlds to see her. She pushed open the front door and rushed outside into the cool night air. Her chest rose and fell with each breath, tears streaked her makeup, and her knees bore the marks of her fall. She kept running, not looking back until her house appeared in the distance. Soon, her sobs grew louder, heartfelt and free, echoing softly along the quiet street.

Then–headlights.

A silver car screeched to a halt a few feet away.

"Liza!" a voice shouted. Leo.

He was out of the car in an instant. One look at her–shaking, crying, torn–and his expression darkened.

"What happened?" he asked, catching her as she staggered into his arms.

She collapsed against him, unable to speak, her hands clutching his shirt as if it were a lifeline.

Leo searched everywhere, his jaw tensing. His eyes turned icy.

"Who did this to you?"

She only sobbed harder in reply.

He carefully draped his coat over her trembling shoulders and quietly led her to the car. Whatever reason had brought him there that night now seemed insignificant, almost absurd in the face of what had just happened. His heart felt heavy, crushed under guilt, regret, and the unbearable truth that he hadn't been there when his sister needed him most. A dozen what-ifs clawed at his mind, each one sharper than the last–if he had come earlier, if he had noticed the signs, if he had chosen differently.

Now, the path ahead looked darker than ever, littered with consequences he could neither foresee nor escape.

And in that moment, something within him shattered quietly but irreparably, as if a piece of his soul had been ripped away.

Chapter 13
The Wrath of Leo Carlos

Liza remained in her room for hours, her sobs escalating into screams that echoed throughout the house. She was overwhelmed with fear and anger, feeling entirely cut off from everything around her. Outside, Leo and Elena watched helplessly, deeply shaken. They had never seen her like this before. Someone had hurt her, and Leo knew that someone would face the consequences.

Liza had always been incredibly determined, carrying the same fiery spirit that once made Leo a formidable fighter in the ring. She was fierce, stubborn, and seemingly untouchable–or so he believed. But that night, everything changed forever.

Finally, the door creaked open. Leo stayed tense on the sofa, watching. Liza emerged–no tears, no fear, only fury blazing in her eyes. She crept to her mother's side, wrapping her arms around Elena and pressing close, finding comfort in the embrace. Her voice was hoarse, raw from hours of weeping. Yet when she spoke, it was steady. One name escaped her lips: Dev Gambhir.

Leo didn't speak. Didn't breathe. Didn't blink.

He sat perfectly still, fists clenched, as each detail she revealed about the party tightened his nerves. The anger within him burned steadily, not as a chaotic blaze but as a sharpened edge, precise and deliberate. It wasn't blind fury or impulsive revenge–it was the cold, measured determination of a man ready to act, weighing each move before striking. Every word she spoke only fuelled that quiet, relentless fire.

This wasn't about power, money, or ego. It was personal.

In the morning, Leo stormed through the magnificent iron gates of Raj Gambhir's hilltop mansion, not bothering to announce himself. His arrival made it clear: he was there without hesitation or any need for permission.

The guards didn't raise their weapons. They recognised him. Leo–former kickboxing champion and ex-enforcer for Lucas Dada, a man notorious for broken bones and unresolved grudges. His name still echoed in whispers through Goa's underworld. He wasn't anyone you challenged; you just watched and hoped he wasn't there for you.

Leo strode through the marble corridors as if he owned them. The mansion was a showcase of luxury–Persian rugs, antique chandeliers, and walls adorned with imported art. Still, Leo didn't even glance at anything else. His focus was solely on the man at the end of the corridor.

Raj Gambhir lounged beneath a grand crystal chandelier, a glass of single malt whisky in one hand and a folded newspaper in the other. A silk robe casually draped over his well-toned frame revealed a glimpse of a tattoo snaking down his collarbone. He looked more like a smug prince than the architect of Goa's criminal empire.

When Raj looked up and saw Leo, he grinned.

"Leo," he said, lounging further into the leather chair as if greeting a casual acquaintance. "Now this is a surprise. You've been keeping a low profile. What brings you here so early in the morning?"

Leo remained silent. His fists clenched at his sides, but his voice was steady—perhaps too steady.

"Your brother," he said, each word precise and deliberate. "He touched my sister, Liza."

The air shifted.

For a moment, the smile on Raj's face paused. His eyes narrowed slightly, showing he had heard and understood. Then, as quickly as it appeared, his expression softened again. He chuckled softly and leaned back, the ice gently tinkling in his glass, adding a touch of relaxed ease to the scene.

"Touched?" Raj echoed, his tone languid and condescending. "Come on, Leo—Dev's just a kid. A bit wild, sure, but he's not a monster. Parties get messy. Lines blur. You know how it is."

Leo moved closer, his jaw tight, his voice low and shaking with rage. "She's covered in bruises," he hissed, each word sharp as a knife. "She was *violated*. Do you have any idea what that means? Do you understand what it's like to see someone you care about broken from the inside out—to look into their eyes and realise a part of them has been torn away forever?"

Raj exhaled through his nose and shook his head with mock pity. "Look, I'm sorry she had a rough night, but your sister's not some wide-eyed innocent. She's been around enough of these circles to know the game. If she didn't want attention, she shouldn't have..."

"Don't," Leo interrupted, his voice low and menacing. "Don't you dare."

Nevertheless, Raj pressed on, his irritating smirk widening. "Dev might have gone a bit over the top. Maybe your sister enjoyed the attention more than she's willing to admit."

That was the moment it happened.

Something inside Leo—something long buried under years of restraint—gave way.

In a quick, fluid motion, he closed the gap, grabbing Raj by the collar. The whisky glass shattered on the floor. Raj gasped, more shocked than hurt.

"You think this is a joke?" Leo growled, his face just inches from Raj's, voice shaking with fury. "You think I came here to talk terms? Dev violated my sister—and you sit there smirking like it means nothing." His fists clenched.

Behind them, a tense atmosphere crackled as the guards shifted nervously, their hands hovering over holsters, ready for action. The room seemed on the brink of chaos. Yet, Raj, unexpectedly calm, raised a single hand—a quiet signal. The guards paused, a flicker of uncertainty in their eyes as they held their stance.

"You have no idea what line you have just crossed, Leo," he stated, his voice now steady and cold.

Leo released him, allowing the robe to crumple against Raj's chest. "I'm not here to scare you," he said. "I'm here to warn you about what's coming next."

Raj narrowed his eyes. "And what's that?"

Leo turned and walked away with the same deliberate steps he had taken to enter. Just before reaching the doorway, he paused and spoke without looking back:

"I'm going to bury your brother."

He had just made up his mind. If Raj wouldn't deliver justice, he'd seize it himself. With that, he vanished into the sunlight.

Leo waited, biding his time and deliberately allowing the rage to sharpen and intensify. But he knew he had to act soon; things needed to fall into place according to his plan before confronting Dev. He waited like a hunter stalking his prey.

Dev was quite the creature of habit–he was arrogant, spoiled, and predictable. He kept going to the same clubs, gambling at the same casinos, and flirting with the same type of women who, despite laughing at his cruelty, still clung to his power. In a city filled with masks and hidden secrets, Dev was quite open about his sins, always surrounded by bodyguards who kept him well protected.

Leo watched him from the shadows, feeling a quiet yet intense fire inside. Each time he saw Dev laugh, toss money onto a table, or hold a woman close, a new wave of anger ignited within him. It's not the kind of rage that makes men shout, but the kind that freezes you in place. The kind that settles deep in your bones and leaves you hollowed out.

He remembered Liza's face—the fear in her eyes, the quiet trembling in her voice as she recounted what Dev had done. She had finished crying and feeling helpless. Yet the brokenness persisted, visible in every pause, every glance at the floor, and every time she pulled her sleeves down despite the bruises already fading.

Leo had spent his life fighting: in the ring, on the streets, against poverty, against fate. Yet nothing he had ever fought for made him feel as helpless as witnessing his sister that night.

Then, Leo realised it was the perfect moment to act. Today was the day he would carry out both of his plans for revenge.

Dev stepped out of the casino just after midnight, slightly tipsy and full of laughter. He had an arm around a woman whose heels softly clicked on the pavement. They shared a quiet giggle into the shadows, slipping behind a row of parked cars. Ten minutes later, the woman cheerfully left, smiling and adjusting her dress, her heels gently clicking as she hopped into a waiting cab.

And Dev, foolish, swaggering Dev, wandered further into the deserted car park alone.

At that moment, Leo stepped out of the shadows like a ghost summoned by Dev's own guilt.

"Dev." He screamed.

The younger Gambhir shifted his gaze. At first, his eyes looked glassy and unfocused. Then, a flicker of recognition appeared, along with a smirk.

"Leo," he said, with a drunken drawl. "What do you want?"

Leo did not respond.

Leo raised the gun, the silencer shimmering in the dim light. His hands were steady, yet inside, a storm raged. Images of Liza's broken face, her screams, her silence–they all collided in his mind. There was no space for mercy, no hesitation.

Dev didn't even flinch.

One shot.

Straight through the skull.

Dev died before he hit the ground.

Silence fell. Not the peaceful kind, but the heavy, resonant type that surrounds your soul and tightens it.

Leo remained still, his gun still raised as he looked at the body. He had anticipated feeling satisfied, relieved, or a sense of emotional release from the rage that had taken hold of him.

But it wasn't there.

Instead, what came was a torrent of memories–sharp, brutal, steeped in blood. Because this wasn't the first time that night, Leo had pulled the trigger.

The first face that flashed before him was that of Albert at the warehouse, who had lunged at him with a knife. That shot had been quick, instinctive, the kind of split-second choice a man makes when survival is all that matters. He hadn't thought twice then; the pounding in his chest had drowned the echo of the gunfire.

Killing Albert was a necessity, a grim transaction of violence in exchange for his own life.

But Dev... Dev was different. There was no loose end. This wasn't self-defence—it was judgment, cold and final. It was justice served from the barrel of a gun.

And yet, even as Leo stared at the body, fury still pulsed within him. No bullet could undo what had been done to Liza. No blood could wash away the guilt Leo felt for not protecting her sooner. He had always been the shield, the older brother, the fighter. And yet, Dev had found a way to hurt her.

Leo had no choice but to disappear, into the mist rolling in from the coast, into the shadows that embraced him like an old friend. The duffel bag slung over his shoulder felt heavier now, burdened not only with the tools of violence but also with the weight of the man he had become.

Once, he was Leo Carlos—Goa's emerging fighter, the man who made his name through sweat and honour. Now, he was something else—an outlaw, a traitor, a shadow of his former self. Leo stood on the edge of a crucial reckoning as the storm started to brew.

And the game was only just beginning.

Chapter 14
The Aftermath: A Blood Feud Begins

Both murders profoundly shocked Goa's criminal circles. Dev was more than just another body in the morgue—it felt like a declaration of war. Meanwhile, Raj Gambhir spiralled into a frenzy.

His brother lay dead—his blood spilt as if it was nothing. Someone had dared to challenge him, to question his authority. Raj's fury was fierce; unlike anything he'd ever experienced before. His hands trembled, not out of fear, but with blazing rage. His vision blurred. His brother—his blood, his anchor—was gone. And he knew Leo would pay for this.

The next day, the funeral was brief, but the fire ignited in Raj's heart would burn forever. Standing beside the pyre, he watched the flames consume his brother's remains. He swore in silence that Leo would suffer a fate far crueller than death.

And for Lucas, the blow was devastating. His most trusted lieutenant was dead. His wealth and secrets had been taken from him. It wasn't just theft; it was a warning. A provocation. A shot was fired directly at his throne.

Lucas, the undisputed king of Goa's underworld, ruled with an iron fist. He had seen men rise and fall, witnessed betrayals, and orchestrated executions. But this was different. This was personal. His grip tightened around his whisky glass as he listened to the reports flooding in. His men, his empire – all at risk because Leo had dared to strike at the very foundation of his power.

Raj was determined to kill him, and Lucas shared that resolve–for they both knew that Leo, daring and recklessly bold, was the only man audacious enough to challenge the untouchable.

For two days, they searched relentlessly across the city, eager to find him. Goa, their vibrant hub and stronghold, transformed into a busy hunting ground. What was once a peaceful sanctuary for tourists and revellers suddenly turned into a tense battleground. The team explored the beaches, lively nightclubs, bustling docks, and hidden alleys. They spoke to informants, offered bribes, and whispered threats in the shadows. Yet, Leo remained unseen–like a ghost slipping away into the night.

Raj's frustration grew with each passing hour, his anger turning into obsession. He could neither eat nor sleep. Every second that Leo remained alive felt like an insult, a knife twisting in his gut. He paced his study like a caged animal, fingers curling into fists, and his jaw clenched so tightly that it ached.

Raj and Lucas never let anything slip past. They never forgot, nor did they forgive.

Raj and Lucas moved swiftly through the streets, turning every corner into a potential trap for Leo. They understood it was only a matter of time before Leo was found and dragged out of whatever hole he had slipped into. When that moment arrived, there would be no mercy, no reprieve, and certainly no quick end. They aimed to make Leo suffer pain and beg for mercy. He would witness everything he loved shatter right before his eyes. In his desperation, he would even wish for death before it all finally reached its conclusion.

They sent out their most trusted men, offering rewards for any clues about Leo's whereabouts. Posters with Leo's face went up in the hidden corners of the underworld, marked with the words "Dead or Alive." The message was direct: betrayal wouldn't be accepted.

Informants were interrogated relentlessly. Anyone suspected of aiding Leo faced harsh consequences. Safe houses were raided, and associates were detained. The city's underworld quivered under the fury of Raj and Lucas.

But Leo remained elusive, like a phantom slipping through their grasp.

Desperation was starting to creep in.

In the past, they had limited their violence to those who played the game—politicians, smugglers, turncoats. But now, the boundaries were becoming blurred. The death of Dev had shattered Raj's world, and the silence from Leo only made things worse. Weeks had passed, and Leo was nowhere to be found. No word, no message, no sign. It was as if he had vanished from the face of the Earth.

But Raj knew better. Leo was still in Goa. He could sense it, smell it in the air.

So, they approached those who stood to lose something.

Liza Carlos, Leo's younger sister, had always been off-limits. Even Lucas, who had orchestrated numerous assassinations, once told Raj, "You don't touch family unless you're ready to bury your own." There was an unspoken rule among the old gangsters: women and children were not collateral unless they were traitors themselves. Dev broke that rule.

They wouldn't hurt Liza, not at this moment. But they would undoubtedly make her aware she was being watched, gently reminding her she wasn't alone.

One evening, as Liza returned from her nursing shift at the local clinic, she sensed it—that invisible tension that clings to the skin like cold sweat. The streets felt unusually silent, and the streetlight outside her flat flickered feebly, as if afraid of what it might reveal.

As she reached her door, she paused. Something felt amiss. A note, folded in half, lay on the doormat. There was no envelope. No name.

Her hands trembled as she opened it.

"Tell your brother to surrender, or you and your mother will face the consequences."

Liza instinctively looked around, but the corridor was empty. The neighbours' doors were shut. The silence was oppressive.

She stepped inside and locked the door. She hurried to her mother and hugged her tightly. Elena was terrified.

Her heart pounded, but her eyes remained dry. Fear tightened her chest, yet she refused to show weakness—neither to Raj, nor to Lucas, nor to anyone.

Taking a deep breath, Liza dialled the number. She understood it wasn't just any call—it was the final one she would ever make.

She understood how vital it was to remain alert, so she often kept her movements unpredictable and carefully avoided being followed. Nonetheless, her paranoia intensified with each passing day, making her feel more anxious but also more resolute in her efforts to stay safe.

Raj and Lucas didn't want them dead—not yet.

Both men understood the chessboard all too well. Killing Liza or Elena might bring them temporary satisfaction, but it would destroy the one advantage they still possessed—leverage. Leo was many things, but he wasn't heartless.

So, they waited and watched.

Every other day, a van stopped outside Liza's house. A man driving it concealed himself behind a newspaper. Each morning, a woman ran past at the same time. It wasn't a coincidence. Liza was under constant surveillance—her routines watched, her movements recorded. Every step, every glance, quietly documented.

Lucas had also stopped by to see the police commissioner, someone he knew pretty well. "Keep them under quiet surveillance," he had said with a relaxed smile, taking a sip of his drink. "Don't intervene. Just let them feel the pressure."

Fear, he believed, would do what bullets couldn't.

Liza and Elena were not ordinary women. They held something rare: a deep trust in Leo and a firm resolve not to be pawns in Raj's game.

They began to notice the watchers around them. There was the familiar man at the chai stall, and that same taxi which made its rounds three times in just an hour. Although they didn't speak to each other, their instincts were in perfect sync, sharing an unspoken understanding.

They knew survival meant only one thing—disappearing without a trace.

Liza and Elena packed a single bag, burned the note she had received, and left their house at 3:15 a.m., locking the door behind them for the final time. Without a backwards glance, they slipped into the hushed Goan night, swallowed by its shadows.

They had prepared for this moment.

On the phone, Leo's voice had been low and urgent: "If things go sideways, there's a place." He hadn't explained, and Liza hadn't dared to ask. But she remembered.

The next morning, Raj's men came pounding at her door. No answer. A swift kick shattered the lock, and the door swung open.

The house was silent. Rooms stripped bare of presence. They were gone–vanished, as if the night itself had swallowed them whole.

Back at Raj's villa, the news landed like a sledgehammer. Lucas's jaw tightened, his eyes burning with fury. He didn't curse, but the silence around him was sharper than any outburst. He dragged on his cigarette one last time before grinding it savagely beneath his heel.

"They were right under our noses!" Raj yelled, slamming his glass against the wall. "You told me to wait, to watch–now they're gone."

Lucas remained silent for a long moment, simply gazing out of the window at the garden below. Then, with a calm demeanour, he said, "They haven't gone far. Leo wouldn't send them out into the world alone. He has them somewhere. And wherever they are... he is too."

Yet deep down, both realised that the moment the women vanished, the game had changed.

Raj and Lucas had lost their bait, and Leo, lurking in the shadows, had just regained control of the board.

As weeks passed without success, tensions between Raj and Lucas started to emerge. Accusations were hurled, and trust began to erode. Their shared aim of catching Leo remained, but their methods started to diverge. Their alliance, once strong, showed signs of strain. The once-united front started to fall apart under the weight of their obsession.

Chapter 15
Detective Aamir: The Man Who Saw Beyond the Obvious

Years later, Leo Carlos had resurfaced. Maddy was dead. Leo had been framed. The past had come full circle. And this time, Raj Gambhir and Lucas Dada would not allow him to escape.

Leo had once vanished into the coastal fog like a ghost, his name whispered in pubs, back alleys, and in the minds of those who remembered the blood-soaked night that shattered the underworld's fragile balance. But time has a way of luring even ghosts back into the light. And this time, Leo was back in the game–only now, the board belonged to someone else.

Raj and Lucas had eagerly anticipated this moment. They had waited, plotted, and built an empire in Leo's absence. Now, at last, everything had fallen into place.

Aamir had built his career on one unshakeable principle: nothing is ever as it seems.

He wasn't flashy. He wasn't loud. But behind his calm exterior lay a mind as sharp as a razor's edge, honed by years of navigating lies, motives, and the smokescreens of power. Aamir didn't believe in simple answers; he dissected them, peeling back layers until he could see the truth writhing beneath.

Inside the department, opinions diverged sharply. Some claimed he had no soul, treating every crime as a puzzle rather than a tragedy. Others swore he was the last man who genuinely cared. But in the underworld, there was no debate—he was a shark in black waters: silent, relentless, built to hunt. Not just a police officer, but a predator among predators. To them, he was fire itself—uncontrollable, consuming, and impossible to outrun.

Aamir's desk was often a vibrant chaos, cluttered with case files, crime scene photographs, and notebooks brimming with coded thoughts. His eyes held a haunted look, reflecting someone who had witnessed a lot but couldn't quite turn away . Something was intriguing, even unsettling, about his instincts.

His timing? Impeccable. He would enter interrogation rooms and remain silent for the first ten minutes—merely observing. And it often proved effective.

He consistently seemed to anticipate five moves in advance. Some regarded him as brilliant; others thought him insane.

A few years ago, when the Maddy Nik case drew everyone's attention and Leo Carlos's name became known, Aamir didn't just see a suspect—he saw an intriguing story waiting to be uncovered. For years, he had been closely observing Leo, Raj, Lucas, Maddy, and their connections in the underground world, quietly collecting clues. Aamir wasn't just a detective; he was a true student of human nature, skilled at noticing subtle cues and uncovering motives in unspoken moments. Every file, interview, and scar revealed part of a deeper story.

He saw a question.

And that was what made him dangerously cautious; once Aamir started to dig, no secret stayed hidden.

Not Leo's.

Not Raj's.

Certainly not Lucas Dada's.

The Early Days: A Detective Unlike Any Other

Aamir never quite fit the mould of a typical police officer. Rules didn't just restrict him; he was focused on achieving results. His approach was unorthodox, sometimes even bordering on illegality, but it always proved successful.

When he first joined the force, his superiors brushed him off as reckless, just another hot-headed rookie. But within a year, he cracked three cases others had long given up on—each tangled, each thought unsolvable. He wasn't after medals or headlines; he was chasing truth. What set him apart were instincts sharp as a blade and skills honed beyond his years—an edge that made him impossible to ignore.

What made Aamir truly exceptional was not just his intelligence—it was his ability to think like a criminal. He understood them; he knew how they moved, how they covered their tracks, and how they concealed themselves in plain sight.

He always dug deeper, seeking the motives behind every crime. Why would someone commit this crime? What might they do next? How could he stay a step ahead? His ability to anticipate his adversaries' moves made him truly formidable. The underworld buzzed with stories about him: "Aamir doesn't chase criminals. He waits for them to act... and he's already there."

Aamir had always been the quiet child in a noisy Lucknow mohalla. While other boys raced kites on rooftops or played gully cricket until dusk, Aamir could often be found sitting on the steps of the old police chowki at the end of the lane, observing. He wasn't playing or talking–just watching.

His mother, Inspector Nazneen Khan, was an imposing figure in his life. She was one of the first women in his family to wear the khaki uniform, carrying herself like a shield of strength. Bold, keen-eyed, and always honest, Nazneen had made many enemies over the years, but she earned a lot of respect, too. Aamir watched her walk confidently through the narrow streets in her neat uniform, commanding respect without words and making others cautious with her intense gaze. Criminals were afraid of her, while ordinary people looked up to her with admiration. For young Aamir, she was like a superhero–not just because she was strong, but because her determination never wavered.

During his childhood, he never needed cartoons or bedtime stories. His mother's files were his fairy tales: murder reports, missing person cases, smuggling dossiers. Nazneen would bring them home, sometimes unintentionally, and Aamir would sneak glances, not for gore or thrills, but for puzzles. He was fascinated by how a story could change depending on whose version you heard, and how a single footprint or misplaced button could unravel a lie.

By the time he was eleven, Aamir had a special gift—he noticed things others overlooked. He had a keen eye for contradictions in conversations, could recall exactly where objects were in a room, and could even tell when someone was pretending to smile. Once, when a neighbour's watch went missing, everyone in the colony immediately blamed the domestic help. But Aamir noticed that the neighbour's son had recently started wearing long sleeves—unusual for a warm May afternoon in Lucknow. It turned out he was hiding a scratch on his wrist from climbing into his father's locked cupboard. The watch was found there, and Aamir chose to stay quiet, not saying "I told you so."

His mother didn't always approve of his nosiness. "You'll grow up paranoid," she would say. But secretly, she was proud. She recognised in him the instincts of a natural cop—one who didn't just chase clues but read between them.

When she died, ambushed during a high-profile investigation into land mafia collusion, Aamir was sixteen. The grief was immense, but it didn't break him; instead, it crystallised something within. That night, sitting beside her ashes, he made a silent vow: he wouldn't merely join the police. He would become the kind of officer who didn't need permission to do what was right.

By his late twenties, Aamir had cleared the civil service exams but chose not to take the easy route of the IAS. Instead, he became an ASP, Goa cadre, and committed to serving in crime intelligence at the ground level. While others advanced up the bureaucratic ladder, he preferred fieldwork. His methods were sometimes unconventional and often looked down upon–but his results demonstrated their effectiveness.

Recognition never mattered to Aamir; what he craved were answers. To him, every crime was a layered deception, a carefully constructed façade. He had spent a lifetime learning to peel back those layers. Raised amid chaos, he understood lies not just as words but as weapons. He knew exactly where to look when the truth was hidden.

The Case of the "Faceless Killer"

One of Aamir's most talked-about cases–the stuff of whispered legend in police circles–was the hunt for the "Faceless Killer." A phantom who struck without leaving a single shred of evidence behind: no DNA, no fingerprints, no witnesses. Just silence and seven lifeless bodies, each found meticulously staged, with the scenes eerily pristine.

The investigation dragged on for six months. Officers came and went. The media lost interest. Leads went cold. It was a dead case–until Aamir took it up.

He began not with the crime scenes but with the victims. He spent weeks analysing their lives—their morning walks, the books they read, the songs they played, the places they lingered. While others searched for connections in blood, Aamir looked at behaviour. Then, buried in the mundane, he discovered a pattern—one tiny thread. Every victim had visited the same nondescript café in the week before they were murdered.

It wasn't a smoking gun, but Aamir never needed one.

For the next fortnight, he became a ghost in that café—blending in with the regulars, sipping the same weak coffee, pretending to read newspapers while his eyes scanned every face. He memorised routines, noted subtle gestures, and waited for the slightest ripple in the pattern.

On the fourteenth day, he saw him.

A man in a grey windbreaker, in his mid-forties, clean-shaven and unremarkable. He arrived precisely at 9:15 a.m. each morning, sat in the furthest corner, ordered nothing, and said nothing to anyone. His gaze never wavered; he wasn't watching anyone, yet somehow, he was intensely aware—too still, too focused. There was a cold, deliberate control in his manner, like a hunter waiting for his moment.

Something about him—his very ability to leave no trace—set off alarm bells deep in Aamir's gut.

He carefully followed him.

The man took winding routes through side streets, doubled back twice, and slipped into alleys with seasoned caution. Aamir remained discreet, making sure not to spook him. Then the suspect realised he was being tailed.

What began as shadowing erupted into a relentless pursuit—through crowded markets, deserted underpasses, and rain-slick overpasses echoing with hurried footsteps.

The chase ended at a decrepit warehouse on the city's edge.

Inside, they circled each other like predators. No guns, no shouting—only silence and tension so thick it felt like glass about to shatter.

Aamir closed in, inch by inch, herding the man toward a pile of abandoned crates. A brief, vicious struggle followed. And then it was over. Aamir slammed the cuffs onto the wrists of the faceless killer.

The man had wiped away every trace of his crimes—but there was one thing he could never erase: Aamir's relentless understanding of human nature.

Aamir didn't just solve the case through lab reports and forensics. He solved it through instinct, forged in fire and sharpened by a lifetime of observation—and by an unyielding hunger for the truth.

—

The Drug Cartel Takedown: Aamir vs. The Cobra Syndicate

The Cobra Syndicate had been one of the most elusive and feared drug cartels in Mumbai and Goa. For over a decade, it had moved like a ghost—shipping narcotics worth millions, corrupting officials in high places, and silencing anyone who dared speak out. Its network was a fortress, its methods ruthless. And its leader? A phantom. No photograph. No fingerprints. Not even a name—just whispers drifting through the underworld.

When Aamir was assigned the case, he refused to chase after drugs like his predecessors. He knew the powder and pills were merely the surface. The real power lay in the money.

For weeks, he dissected financial ledgers and sifted through layers of shell companies, suspicious invoices, and offshore accounts. Hidden among them, he uncovered a trail leading back to a prestigious estate firm with extensive holdings in Goa and Dubai. On paper, everything appeared impeccable. But Aamir sensed the decay beneath the glossy exterior.

He decided to strike back. He crafted a trap—a phantom shipment worth ₹500 crores, a tantalising bait meant to draw the syndicate out of hiding. Word of the fake consignment slipped into the proper channels, and Aamir waited.

It didn't take long.

Within days, the syndicate made its move. Disguised as customs officials, their operatives swooped in to seize the phantom cargo at a private dockyard under cover of darkness.

What they didn't know was that Aamir and his team had already transformed the entire port into a fortress of hidden cameras, wiretaps, and sharpshooters waiting in the shadows.

When the syndicate struck, the trap quickly shut, unleashing chaos. Gunshots rang out through the salty air, and searchlights scanned over crates and shipping containers. Within just a few minutes, thirty-four men were caught, stunned and feeling cornered.

But the true revelation lay beyond the arrests.

For the first time, the syndicate's elusive leader stepped out of the shadows—a respected businessman who had navigated Goa's upper circles for years, shaking hands at charity galas and dining with politicians, his true identity hidden behind charm and influence.

Aamir had not merely dismantled a drug ring. He had torn away the mask of a man who had ruled the underworld undetected for a decade.

Ransom – Aamir vs. Human Trafficking

It began as a straightforward ransom case. Eight-year-old Rohan Malhotra was abducted from his school bus in broad daylight, vanishing as if swallowed by the earth itself. The kidnappers had been thorough—no security footage, no fingerprints, and no witnesses able to provide a helpful description. The police searched for leads, while the pressure grew from Rohan's father, a powerful politician whose fury shook the corridors of power.

That was when Aamir was called in.

He hadn't spent a moment chasing false leads. Instead, he concentrated on the ransom note—a demand so outrageously high and brazen that it seemed less driven by greed and more by arrogance. Aamir sensed this was no ordinary crime.

He examined the phone records, analysing the pattern of the burner numbers used for the ransom calls. After countless hours of tracking digital traces, one number finally led him to a neglected warehouse on the outskirts of the city. Inside, he found grim clues—discarded food wrappers, fibres from ropes, and faint traces of chloroform lingering in the air. Rohan had been there. But he was gone.

Refusing to lose momentum, Aamir set his own trap. He leaked false intelligence suggesting the ransom money was ready, waiting at a secluded drop point. He stationed undercover officers at every possible exit, waiting in the shadows.

The kidnappers took the bait.

When one of them arrived under the cover of darkness, Aamir swooped in. Under the searing glare of interrogation lights and relentless questioning, the man finally broke, spilling a truth far more sinister than anyone had imagined.

This hadn't been just a simple kidnapping. It was only a cover—a smokescreen for a vast human trafficking network, snatching children to be routed through secret channels and delivered to an elite clientele willing to pay any price. Rohan had been one child among many, destined for a fate too terrible to imagine.

Aamir moved swiftly, assembling a strike team and launching an assault on the traffickers' secret HQ. The raid turned violent–gunfire rang through tight passageways, traffickers tried to run, and terrified children hid in corners.

When the dust finally settled, Rohan was rescued, trembling but alive. Dozens of traffickers were taken away in handcuffs, and an empire of darkness was torn apart.

For Aamir, solving the case had never been about rescuing just one child. It had been about destroying an entire industry built on stolen lives–a victory not merely of law, but of humanity itself.

—

The Frame-Up: When Aamir Met Leo Carlos

Now, Aamir was staring at a very different kind of case.

A murder.

A setup.

A tangled web of crime, revenge, and deception that stinks of power plays and buried secrets.

And at the heart of it all?

Leo Carlos.

The name alone carries weight–infamy, myth. Leo is the kind of man whom people either admire or fear–sometimes both. A fallen fighter turned underworld enigma, Leo vanished into the shadows of Goa's criminal underworld after a bloody chapter closed years ago. Now, he has reappeared, and almost instinctively, a body has followed.

Maddy Nik–the wild card–was dead. And Leo, the man already burdened with too many ghosts trailing him, was the one holding the match.

Or so it appears.

But Aamir didn't believe it. Not even for a moment.

He had reviewed Leo's file. He was aware of the past–the murders, the vendettas, the disappearances. Yet he also understood how Leo moves: quietly, calculated, controlled. This crime scene, by contrast, screams of something else entirely. It was too clean, too precise, too eager to blame.

And Aamir has seen enough frame-ups to recognise one.

The body was arranged like a performance. The fingerprint on the glass, the lack of resistance, and the hotel's conveniently broken CCTV–none of it matched Aamir's understanding of spontaneous violence. This wasn't chaos; this was choreography.

Aamir had interviewed Leo once, many years ago–briefly, off the record, during a smuggling investigation that fell apart due to lack of evidence. What he remembered wasn't Leo's silence, but his eyes. They weren't the eyes of a man who enjoys violence. They were the eyes of a man who endures it, lives with it, and knows when to fight–and when to vanish.

Leo was no saint; yet, he wasn't a killer.

Not this killer.

This crime had been sown like a seed, meant to grow quickly and overshadow any truth Aamir might seek to uncover. And that could only mean one thing–someone influential wants Leo gone.

He already had two names in mind.

Raj Gambhir.

Lucas Dada.

Raj, the businessman with a politician's smile and a cobra's patience. And Lucas, the ghost who ruled Goa's underworld with silence and shadows. Together, they control more than just money and guns; they control narratives, courts, and the police.

But Aamir was afraid of nothing except failure. Because if there was one thing Aamir understood better than most, it is this: every lie leaves a footprint. Every truth leaves a trail.

And he would follow this one all the way to the end, even if it meant bringing Goa's darkest figures into the light–even if it meant saving a man whom the world has already condemned.

Leo was fighting not merely for his innocence but for his very life.

And Detective Aamir? He never gave up until he uncovered the truth, no matter who tried to hide it.

Chapter 16
A Web of Lies

Detective Aamir had spent years questioning criminals, dismantling alibis, and exposing carefully constructed façades. He had seen men lie with steady hands and innocent smiles, and he had watched killers crumble under the weight of their guilt. He understood the tricks – the nervous tics of a guilty person, the excessive calm of someone rehearsed in deception, the misplaced confidence of those who believed they were untouchable.

Yet here, in this exclusive coastal resort, where wealth and power gathered under one roof, something felt amiss.

It appeared that honesty was scarce.

Aamir sensed it the moment he arrived. It hung in the air, heavy with the scent of salt and unease – the kind of tension that arises when people aren't afraid of being caught but are terrified of what might happen if they speak the truth.

Some guests eagerly shared their thoughts, hoping to influence the investigation in a specific direction, while others earnestly insisted, they hadn't seen or heard anything. The room was filled with a tense silence, heavy with unspoken fear. Aamir understood the subtle difference between genuinely not knowing and deliberately concealing the truth.

And this? This wasn't just an absence of information—it was a conscious decision to withhold it.

Aamir had already thoroughly examined the crime scene. He observed Maddy's peaceful-looking body lying on the immaculate floor of the suite, her death oddly neat and precise. Usually, a crime of passion is characterised by swift, impulsive actions and intense emotions. But this? This was something quite different and unsettling.

She had been silenced.

As he moved through the resort, Aamir observed everything: the way staff kept their heads down, whispering when they thought no one was watching; the manner in which some guests laughed too loudly, their cheer forced—a mask for their discomfort; and how others avoided his gaze, their eyes flickering away the moment he turned towards them.

They were hiding something.

But what?

The Bartender's Clue

Arun, the bartender, had worked at the resort for many years. He recognised all the important guests, every whispered conversation, and every disagreement.

As Aamir leaned against the polished mahogany counter, watching the man pour a drink for a nervous guest, he realised that Arun had noticed something.

"Long night?" Aamir asked casually. Arun smirked. "Always is."

Aamir placed a photograph on the counter–a grainy image of a man in a sharp suit, jaw clenched, fury in his eyes. He had obtained it from a security guard earlier.

"Do you recognise him?"

Arun exhaled, slowly wiping the counter with deliberate strokes. "Yeah," he admitted. "That's Munna Patel."

Aamir's eyes narrowed. Munna Patel. A notorious enforcer for Raj Gambhir.

"He was here last night?" Arun nodded, lowering his voice. "Came in late. Ordered whisky, neat. Kept looking around, like he was waiting for someone."

Aamir already knew Leo was at the bar before he returned to his suite. "And?"

Arun hesitated, looking around before proceeding. "Maddy came in not long after Leo left. I didn't think much of it at first. But then... Munna approached her. Began whispering something."

He narrowed his eyes. "Whispering or arguing?"

Arun exhaled. "It was quiet at first. But then I saw Maddy push his hand away. She looked angry. Next thing I know, he's gripping her wrist, saying something low and fast."

Aamir's fingers drummed against the counter. An argument. A confrontation. Just before Maddy died.

"What happened next?"

"She pulled away. Walked out of the bar in a hurry." Arun leaned in. "And Munna? He followed her."

That was the break Aamir needed.

—

The Guards' Reluctance

The security team had been quite unhelpful—remarkably so, in fact.

Aamir had already questioned three of them, and their replies were the same. There was nothing suspicious. I didn't notice anything unusual. Maddy entered alone and left alone.

Lies.

Aamir continued, nodding and taking notes to show his attentiveness. Still, he couldn't help but notice the way their eyes flicked around and how their hands clenched at their sides, revealing the fear they felt. It was obvious they were scared.

Not of him. Of something else. Or someone.

The guests were just as bad.

Some had been partying, while others were too drunk to recall anything useful. But Aamir knew that not everyone was entirely oblivious.

One couple, seated on the terrace facing the entrance, had given an alibi so rehearsed that it was almost theatrical.

"We were in our room all night."

Except they hadn't been.

Aamir reviewed the CCTV footage. The woman had left around the same time Maddy had departed from the bar.

Why lie about something so simple?

They possessed a deeper understanding, accompanied by a sense of fear that restrained them.

Aamir had spent enough years on the force to recognise when a murder was personal and when it was a message. Maddy's death wasn't just another crime of passion, a drunken brawl gone fatal, or an impulsive act of rage. No—this was calculated. Planned. Executed with precision.

And, more importantly, it reeked of power. Whoever killed Maddy was not merely an ordinary criminal. They wielded influence—enough to silence people, make witnesses forget what they saw, and even cause the resort staff, usually thriving on gossip, to walk on eggshells.

Aamir saw it in their eyes: the darting glances, the stammered responses, the forced smiles. They were hiding something—they were terrified.

And that fear conveyed one thing to him: Maddy hadn't just been killed; she had been silenced.

Munna Patel: A Crack in the Narrative

Arun, the bartender, had let something slip—something that no one else had brought up.

A man argued with Maddy after Leo left the bar. The argument was briefly heated, but it left a lasting impression. Now, that name was at the centre of Aamir's thoughts.

Munna Patel.

Not a major figure in the underworld, but certainly not unknown either. He was a fixer, an intermediary – one of those people who thrived in the shadows, making sure that certain things happened while others did not. If something needed to be cleaned up, hidden, or "taken care of," Munna was the man people called.

And yet, there was a twist–Munna was seen arguing with Maddy. That was unusual for him. Munna never got emotional; he didn't cause scenes. He worked behind the scenes, not in the spotlight.

That raised a new question.

Aamir watched Arun closely, noticing how the man fidgeted behind the bar, his fingers clutching the rag a little too tightly. He seemed anxious. Too anxious. He approached Arun once more to start another conversation.

"You saw Munna arguing with her," Aamir repeated, his tone calm yet firm. "Did you hear what it was about?"

Arun hesitated. "No."

Aamir raised an eyebrow. "You expect me to believe that? A man argues with a woman in the middle of your bar, voices raised, and you don't hear a word?"

Arun swallowed, eyes darting around the bar as if searching for an escape. "I–I wasn't paying attention, sir."

Aamir leaned in slightly. "That's a lie."

Silence.

Then, after a moment, a whisper arose. "I heard him say, 'You don't understand what you're doing, Maddy.'"

Aamir's sharp gaze was fixed on the bartender. "What did she say?" Arun hesitated once more, and when he finally spoke, his voice was barely above a whisper.

"She said, 'I'm done being scared.'"

Aamir felt a chill run down his spine.

Maddy had been afraid of something or someone. But whatever fear had kept her silent all those years, she had finally decided to break free. And now, she was dead.

Aamir did not believe in coincidences. If Maddy was about to reveal something and Munna had warned her, then either he had murdered her to silence her... or someone else had ensured Maddy would never speak out.

And that was the problem.

Munna was missing.

Aamir wasted no time. He sent officers to track down Munna and search his known hangouts and regular meeting spots. If Munna had killed Maddy, he was either on the run or already dead.

Because if he was not the one to pull the trigger, then whoever did would have ensured that Munna did not live long enough to speak.

And Aamir was not going to let that happen.

Chapter 17
A Clue in the Waves – A New Body, A New Mystery

Detective Aamir faced Leo across the dimly lit suite, the space between them heavy with unspoken tension. The former kickboxer maintained a controlled composure, but Aamir, who had spent years reading people, was not easily fooled. Beneath that tough exterior, Leo was a man teetering on the brink of rage, desperation, or something even darker.

Aamir recognised that expression: men who had endured relentless struggles, men who had perfected the art of masking their pain with calmness even as their inner fire threatened to overwhelm everything. The detective was cautious about jumping to conclusions. Still, something in Leo's posture, in the almost imperceptible shift of his weight, suggested that the man was weighing his next move carefully.

Aamir edged nearer, his voice steady and intentionally probing. "Do you know Raj Gambhir?"

Leo's reaction was immediate. A flicker of recognition–so brief that a less keen investigator might have missed it–but Aamir saw it. The slight tightening of the jaw, the way his fingers curled as if bracing for an unseen blow. It wasn't just recognition; it was something more profound.

Anger? Fear? Hatred? Perhaps all three.

Outside, lightning split the sky, casting jagged shadows across the suite. For a moment, the flash illuminated Leo's face, emphasising the lines of tension around his eyes. It was all Aamir needed to confirm that Raj was more than just a passing acquaintance. He was someone significant.

"I've heard of him," Leo says finally, his tone deceptively casual. Too casual. The kind of forced indifference that only comes when someone is trying too hard to downplay something.

Aamir isn't convinced. He crosses his arms and fixes Leo with a steady stare. "Raj isn't just a businessman. He's a problem solver. The kind of man you don't just 'hear of.' You either work with him, owe him, or you're on his bad side."

Leo exhales and runs a hand through his hair. The slow, deliberate movement is an unconscious attempt to regain control of the conversation. His eyes flicker toward the window as if contemplating an exit before finally settling back on Aamir.

"Raj and I…". He pauses. "We have a history".

Aamir raises an eyebrow. "History, huh? The sort that gets people killed?"

Leo's jaw clenches, yet he stays silent. The silence serves as an adequate response. Aamir can tell–Leo isn't just hiding something; he's protecting something. Or someone.

Before Aamir can press on, the suite door swings open suddenly, crashing against the wall with such force that it jolts both men.

A young constable, barely in his twenties, staggers inside, panting, his sweat-soaked uniform clinging to him. His chest heaves as he struggles to breathe, his wide eyes darting between the detective and Leo.

"Sir–" he gasps, his voice trembling. "There's been another murder."

The atmosphere in the room crackles with tension.

Aamir's eyes narrow. "Where?"

"The beach," the constable manages, still struggling to steady his breathing. "It's Munna Patel, sir. His throat... was slit."

For a brief moment, neither of them moves.

Leo stiffens. His expression remains unchanged, but Aamir notices how his shoulders tense slightly and his muscles tense as if bracing for a blow.

Munna, the last person to have seen Maddy alive, was the only man who could have shed light on this tangled web they face. And now, he is dead.

Aamir's mind races. This isn't a coincidence. Someone is tying up loose ends. First Maddy, now Munna. Whoever is behind this is systematic and precise. They aren't merely killing for the thrill–they are removing potential threats.

Aamir turns to Leo. "You're coming with me."

Leo's eyes darken, but he doesn't argue.

Without another word, they hurry out of the suite and follow the constable through the resort's winding corridors. Outside, the storm has subsided, although distant thunder still rolls, providing a constant backdrop to the tense atmosphere.

By the time they reach the beach, a small crowd has gathered, including hotel staff, security personnel, and a few lingering tourists drawn by the commotion. The flashing lights of police vehicles cast eerie shadows over the sand, turning the shoreline into a crime scene.

Munna's body lies sprawled on the wet sand, the tide creeping dangerously close to his lifeless form. His throat has been slit cleanly, a deep, precise cut, evidence of expertise rather than recklessness. Blood has seeped into the sand, darkening it beneath his body. His eyes are still open, frozen in an expression of terror.

Aamir crouches beside the body, examining the scene carefully. There are no signs of a struggle or defensive wounds. Either Munna was entirely caught off guard, or he recognised his killer.

Leo stands a few feet away, his expression unreadable. Yet Aamir senses the tension emanating from him.

The detective looks up at his constable. "Witnesses?"

The young officer shakes his head. "None so far, sir. No one saw anything. Or at least, no one is admitting to it."

Aamir exhales sharply. Same pattern. Lies. Half-truths. Fear hangs in the air like a dense fog.

His gaze flickers towards the distant resort buildings, where the warm glow of lights seems almost mocking against the harsh, brutal reality before him.

Someone at that resort is involved in a risky game. If Aamir doesn't start piecing the clues together soon, Leo might be the one left to take the blame.

He glances down at Munna's lifeless body once more, his mind already considering the possibilities.

Whoever is responsible for this has not yet finished. And Aamir is short on time.

Leo stands a short distance away, silent and inscrutable. Aamir doesn't miss how his fists clench.

"You knew him?" Aamir asks, his voice low.

Leo exhales, gazing at the body. "I knew of him."

"That's not what I asked."

Leo's gaze meets Aamir's. "Yeah," he admits. "I knew him."

Aamir turns back to the corpse. "And now he's dead."

A wave of suspicion sweeps through him. Munna has been the missing link—the last known person to have seen Maddy alive. If he had any answers, they have been silenced.

This is not random. This is a clean-up.

Someone wants Munna dead before he can speak.

—

The Message in Blood

Aamir stood, surveying the area. The murder had been brutal yet efficient—a professional's work.

There were no signs of a struggle. No footprints led away. Whoever committed this knew how to vanish.

He turned to one of the forensic officers who had just arrived. "Check his pockets. See if anything was left behind."

A young officer was carefully searching Munna's clothing. He retrieves a small, folded piece of paper, now soaked in water and blood.

Aamir took it, carefully unfolding the damp paper. Though the writing was smudged, it remained legible.

"Too late, Detective. Leo is next."

Aamir's jaw tightens. He has faced many killers in his career—some reckless, others meticulous. But this? This feels entirely different. This is someone who isn't just one step ahead of the investigation but is actively pulling the strings, making sure Aamir knows it.

He looks at Leo and turns his gaze back to Munna's lifeless body. The wound is clean and precise—a single deep cut across the throat, severing the carotid artery. A quick kill. No unnecessary bloodshed beyond what is required. No sign of hesitation. The killer had walked right up to Munna, done what needed to be done, and vanished without a trace.

Aamir examines the surrounding sand. No footprints lead away. The rain and tide might have erased any signs, or perhaps the killer had taken precautions. Either way, it is obvious: whoever did this is experienced. A professional.

Someone has foreseen his arrival. This isn't just a murder–it is a message.

A challenge.

He turns to Leo. "Still think this has nothing to do with you?"

Leo doesn't answer.

Because he knows, just as Aamir does, that this is only the beginning.

Chapter 18
The Betrayal

Detective Aamir stood on the rain-drenched pavement, the salty breeze from the sea blending with the faint metallic smell of blood that remained at the crime scene. The constant hum of the waves crashed against the shore, indifferent to the violence that had unfolded only hours earlier.

Munna's body had already been taken to the morgue, but his death left more than just a corpse—it left behind questions.

Why now?

Why was Munna murdered now, after living in the shadows for years, keeping his head down, earning his money, and staying out of trouble?

Aamir had been a detective long enough to understand that coincidences did not exist in murder investigations. The calculated nature of the killings, the precision of the execution, and the looming shadow of Raj Gambhir and Lucas Dada all pointed to something far more complex than a simple crime of opportunity.

Aamir had devoted years to catching criminals, uncovering their webs of deception, and tracing trails of blood and secrets. But this case was more than just greed or revenge. It was like a complex puzzle—a twisted, meticulously planned game where every move was calculated with purpose.

And at the heart of everything?

Leo Carlos.

Leo stood a few feet away, arms crossed over his chest, his face an unreadable mask. The man radiated a kind of stillness Aamir had come to recognise–controlled, practised, dangerous.

But Aamir wasn't looking at the mask.

He was observing the details.

There was a slight tension in Leo's jaw. His fingers twitched before curling into a fist, as if resisting the urge to react. His gaze lingered–perhaps a moment too long–on the sand where Munna had bled out.

This wasn't surprising.

It was recognition. Leo understood something.

Aamir had spent years dismantling criminals, exposing their lies, and uncovering their truths. He recognised the signs–the hesitation before a half-truth, the flicker of calculation in their eyes, and the way their bodies betrayed the words their mouths failed to articulate.

At that moment, Leo was screaming at him silently.

Leo wasn't just connected to this; he was the reason behind it.

Aamir knew one thing for sure: Leo wasn't fleeing from a past mistake; he was at war with it. A war he had tried to escape for five years, a war that had finally caught up with him once more. The only question remaining was—would he survive it this time?

Maddy's death was more than simply another crime scene; it conveyed a message.

She was neither an innocent bystander nor a random casualty. She knew too much. She had been part of Leo's past, intricately woven into the same treacherous world of power, betrayal, and deception.

But Maddy had always managed to stay one step ahead.

She had shaped her life on the edge, skillfully balancing the excitement of crime with the stability of fame. She moved within élite circles, her beauty and talent hiding the secrets she kept.

For years, she had navigated the game shrewdly—never too deep, never too exposed.

Until now, when something had changed. Someone had forced her hand.

Aamir realised that people like Maddy did not just become scared without reason. It was clear she had been searching for something—or someone.

She had felt nervous and restless. A woman who had once been in control suddenly lost her grip. And then—she was dead.

Maddy's murder was not a crime of passion; it was calculated. Precise. There were no signs of forced entry, suggesting she knew her attacker—or at least, she had willingly let them in. Her last known call? To Munna Patel.

That call linked her death to his.

Initially, Aamir regarded him as a suspect—after all, he was the last person seen with Maddy alive, possibly a jealous lover, or perhaps an accomplice who had betrayed her.

But everything changed when Munna was discovered dead, redirecting the entire course of events.

Munna wasn't precisely a mastermind.

He was not a key player like Raj Gambhir or Lucas Dada.

He was a survivor—an under-the-radar hustler who had made a living by knowing when to speak and when to stay silent.

And yet, someone had gone to the trouble of silencing him. This indicated he knew something significant.

Something worth killing for.

Aamir had seen a great deal over his years as a detective—but this was personal.

Tucked inside Munna's pocket was a small, folded piece of paper.

Just two sentences. "Too late, Detective. Leo is next."

A taunt. A warning. A threat. Someone was playing this game on their own terms—and they wanted Aamir to know it.

The Evidence That Tied It All Together

Detective Aamir realised that solving a case is more than just spotting one shard in a cracked mirror; it's about noticing that tiny spark of truth others might overlook. This spark was buried deep beneath years of dirt, deception, and silence, waiting to be uncovered.

The crime scene was nearly perfect. Maddy's hotel room had been thoroughly cleaned–completely free of fingerprints, DNA, or any sign of forced entry, and the surveillance system was carefully erased. It was clear a professional had been involved. However, even the most experienced can make mistakes. Aamir's role was to identify any errors they might have overlooked.

He stood in his office, surrounded by whiteboards filled with timelines, photographs, and location markers. Red strings connected incidents spanning five years–from the night of the missing fortune to Munna's sudden death and Maddy's mysterious death. It appeared chaotic to most, but to Aamir, it was a living puzzle.

Then, a breakthrough.

The Burner Phone.

It started as a routine check–reviewing call logs from Munna's final hours. Most were unremarkable, but one number caught attention. It was a burner, unregistered and prepaid, used only twice: once on the night five years ago when a smuggling operation went wrong and the stolen diamonds disappeared, and the second time just five minutes before Munna was found dead at the resort.

Such coincidences did not exist in Aamir's world; it was a clue—no, a breadcrumb.

The forensic team salvaged what they could. The SIM card had been removed and destroyed, and the battery had been fried, yet they managed to extract fragments of GPS data. It was located within a five-kilometre radius of the resort where Munna died—the same resort where Maddy had spent her final days. Aamir's instincts flared. This wasn't random. It was deliberate. A ghost from the past reaching into the present.

He pushed deeper.

Second clue: The Whisky Glass

Back at the hotel crime scene, Aamir had ordered a thorough check—not just for prints or DNA, but also for trace chemicals. The toxicology report on Maddy indicated signs of a rare sedative called *Calmorin-Z*, a compound not typically found on the street. It was used in high-end psychiatric clinics—difficult to obtain, and even harder to trace. One facility had reported a missing vial the week before Maddy's death: a private clinic in Dona Paula, where Lucas Dada had once financed a wing in his daughter's name.

The whisky glass on Maddy's table—thought to have been wiped—held microscopic residues of the drug. Although not sufficient to provide a traceable dose, it was enough to suggest it had been tampered with. Someone had sedated her.

Someone who knew how to cover their tracks.

Third clue: The Laptop

Leo had secretly handed it over to Aamir only after thoroughly checking it. When they found it hidden beneath the cushion in Maddy's hotel room, it looked old, scratched, and was password-protected. Still, Leo trusted Aamir completely, believing it was important. The tech team unlocked it in just a few minutes.

Inside were folders cryptically labelled "Blue_Rose," "Cargo_Night," and "Delta_House." Most files were corrupted, but one video played. It was surveillance footage—grainy yet usable. It showed Maddy, alone in her room, pacing nervously. She picked up a phone, made a call, and then glanced towards the door.

Someone entered.

The camera was placed at an awkward angle. Light from the hallway obscured the figure, but the silhouette remained clear. Tall. Broad-shouldered. Confident.

Lucas Dada.

Aamir paused the footage, noting the timestamp—exactly 11:50 PM, just minutes before her death. The footage cut off abruptly, but it was enough. If Lucas had been in that room, the drug would not have been an accident; it was a cleanup, a cover-up.

Fourth clue: The Transaction Log

Using the same laptop, the forensic team retrieved hidden financial records—an encrypted ledger that outlined a series of small, irregular bank transfers made to a shell company registered in Hong Kong. The name on the receiving end? **R.G. Holdings.**

Raj Gambhir's fictitious company.

Aamir traced the financial trail. One transaction, from six months before Maddy's death, matched a deposit into a now-closed account linked to her. She had either been paid off or silenced. In any case, she had known something – something significant enough to warrant being silenced.

Fifth clue: The Security Keycard

At the resort, a partial record of digital keycard entries remained even after deletion. It was missed because the entries seemed incomplete. However, Aamir noticed something unusual: Room 120—Maddy's room—had been accessed twice that night, once with her card and once using a master override key.

Only six people had access to the master keys. They included three resort staff members, two maintenance engineers, and one VIP guest staying in the penthouse that night—Raj Gambhir.

Aamir corroborated the staff alibis. Everyone was accounted for.

That left Raj.

The Case Tightened.

Burner phone. Poisoned whisky. Laptop footage. Financial transactions. Keycard access. Like stepping stones across a poisoned river, each piece led to the next. At the other end stood the two men who had always stayed one step ahead—Lucas Dada and Raj Gambhir.

But now, they had created a trail.

One that led through Maddy. Through Munna.

And back to the night five years ago when everything fell apart.

Aamir stood over his evidence board, staring at their photos.

Raj wore his smug corporate smile. Lucas bore a wolfish glare. They had played God for far too long.

Framed Leo. Broken lives. Stolen empires. They were prepared to finish what they had begun.

Raj wanted Leo to suffer before he died. Lucas wished the past erased. Together, they had waited for the perfect moment to strike. And now, they believed that moment had come.

However, the tide was beginning to turn.

Aamir circled the burner phone in red and marked through all the events it had been contacted about.

He whispered to himself, "You can erase fingerprints, delete files, scare witnesses. But you can't erase a pattern."

And what of Aamir? He was a man who lived for patterns.

They made one critical mistake: they framed Leo. In doing so, they awakened the only man who was mad enough—and clever enough—to sift through the wreckage they believed they had buried.

Aamir now understood the message. Framing Leo wasn't just an act of revenge; it was a strategic move. If Leo were convicted of Maddy's murder, all investigations into her case would stop. The media would portray her as a scorned lover, while the diamonds—or drugs, or money—would remain a mystery. The case would be closed.

However, they had underestimated two people.

Leo Carlos. And Detective Aamir.

Since the past never stays hidden, no matter how deep the grave, the truth always manages to surface again.

Aamir turned to Leo, his voice low but firm.

"Tell me the truth, Leo. What happened five years ago?"

Five Years Ago: The fateful night

Raj Gambhir, renowned for his ruthless and cunning personality, was a businessman who operated within questionable legal limits and showed no tolerance for failure. Those working for Raj were expected to achieve results regardless of any shortcomings. In contrast, Lucas Dada represented a starkly different archetype; he was a street king, a crime boss, and a man who influenced Leo's upbringing before discarding him like a worn-out tool. He played a crucial role in teaching Leo not only how to fight but also how to endure hardship and instigate confrontation.

The money had disappeared. The diamonds, the documents, and the hard drives that could implicate Lucas—everything was gone.

Then Dev Gambhir had to die. Leo had sworn to that.

Because that night wasn't just about anger; it was also about vengeance.

Dev—Raj's younger brother, his protégé, the man who had tried to ruin Leo's sister's life—had walked free. Protected by Raj's influence, he remained untouchable beneath Lucas's shadow.

A single bullet to the head. Clean. Efficient. Ruthless.

As soon as Dev hit the ground, everything changed. Gunfire rang out. Chaos spread through the night. But Leo had already moved. He knew where the diamonds were. He knew where the hard drives were hidden. He understood that Lucas Dada, the man who had once treated him like a son, had built his empire on secrets. And those secrets were now in Leo's hands.

For months after that night, the streets buzzed with speculation.

Some claimed that Leo had been set up, betrayed by someone within the operation and forced to flee. Others believed he had orchestrated the entire affair himself—that the calm, calculating fighter had finally outsmarted the very masters who had once dominated him.

One thing was evident. Raj Gambhir was furious. Lucas Dada was even more incensed.

Both of them found themselves caught in a whirlwind of chaos as they desperately tried to recover what was lost and understand how their carefully thought-out plans fell apart. Despite their persistent search and sending out many associates, Leo still managed to disappear without leaving a single trace.

For the next five years, he stayed invisible.

No arrests, no street rumours about him making moves. Nothing at all.

It was as if Leo Carlos had ceased to exist.

But in truth, he was busy rebuilding, working hard behind the scenes.

He used everything he had stolen that night, every treasure he had taken, to build a new life. A life separate from Raj Gambhir. Away from Lucas Dada. Away from the world that had shaped him.

He became legitimate, or at least, sufficiently so.

Investments. Businesses. Real estate. Leo became a success story. He was a man who fought his way up, cleaned the grime from his hands, and made something respectable of himself.

But there was one problem. Men like Raj and Lucas never forget.

They wait. They watch. They knew Leo had taken what they had lost that night. And they knew one day, he would slip up.

Leo didn't reply right away. He looked at the ocean, watching the waves crash like silent witnesses to everything that had occurred.

Then, he exhaled.

"I took it," he says quietly. "I took everything."

Aamir feels his pulse quicken. This is it.

"Where is it now?" Aamir presses.

Leo's jaw clenches. 'I buried it. And now, they want it back."

Aamir swore under his breath.

Raj and Lucas weren't killing for sport. They were cleaning up.

And Leo? He was next.

What struck Aamir was this: neither Raj nor Lucas had acted against Leo immediately.

They possessed the power and the reach.

If they genuinely wanted him dead, they could have arranged it years ago. So why wait five years?

Aamir was starting to realise. They weren't after Leo's life. Not yet. They wanted something more valuable. They sought what he had stolen. Maybe it wasn't just money. Perhaps it was something even greater.

Documents? Evidence? Something so crucial that Raj and Lucas couldn't risk losing it? Whatever it was, it had been worth five years of patience.

And now, they had finished waiting.

Aamir realised that time was slipping away from him.

And if Leo didn't give them what they wanted? Another body would fall.

But Aamir was not willing to let that occur. This was no longer about stolen money or power; it was about survival.

Leo had always known this would end in bloodshed. He had spent five years fleeing, waiting, and observing. But now, the moment had arrived. It was time to bring this to an end–on his own terms. But to do that, he needed to make the next move before they did. And he was prepared for it.

Lucas Dada and Raj had spent years believing they were invincible, thinking that no one could outwit them. Yet, their biggest weakness was often their greed and arrogance. They saw themselves as the predators, never realising that even hunters can become the prey.

And Leo was ready to show them exactly that.

Chapter 19
The Trap is Set

Leo had spent years on the run, blending into the shadows and staying ahead of the system. But he didn't get this far by chance. He succeeded because he had mastered the art of thinking like his enemies–and then, even more skillfully, outsmarting them.

After Maddy's murder and Munna's silence, everything began to clear up. It wasn't just about tying up loose ends; it felt like a way to strengthen their hold, clear the past, and boldly move forward. Raj and Lucas had gone beyond just seeking revenge; they aimed to wipe out the very legend of Leo Carlos.

But Leo wasn't ready to die.

He had learned from the best–Lucas himself, the man who had once mentored him in Goa's underworld. Leo looked back on those days with mixed feelings–how Lucas had praised him for being fearless, calculating, and efficient. And Raj? Raj had always been a bit jealous, often acting paranoid. He never liked the close bond between Leo and Lucas. Not when Leo was the golden boy. Not after Dev was killed. And especially not when Leo decided to walk away, leaving behind two bodies and an empire in chaos.

However, now that both men were back on the warpath, Leo saw a chance to bring it all to a close finally.

He returned to the files Maddy had gathered before her death, retrieved from the laptop he'd managed to take from her room after the murder. Every page, every note, he combed through with painstaking care, searching for the smallest detail–before finally handing it over to Aamir.

She had been looking into Raj's financial networks–shell companies, shipping documents, and offshore transfers. She wasn't just trying to find justice; she wanted to gain an advantage. Leo found a folder she had stored on an encrypted drive: it contained names, locations, payments, and most importantly, coordinates of past drop points and hidden assets.

What caught his eye was an abandoned warehouse by the docks–once used to store black-market arms during port smuggling operations about ten years ago. It had no official records, no security guards–just sturdy concrete walls, rusted iron gates, and memories that ran deep with blood.

It was perfect.

Leo gazed at the map beneath the flickering light of a desk lamp. His fingers traced the dockside lane before tapping on the warehouse.

This was the point where it had to come to an end.

He sank into the chair, the faint hum of the air conditioner filling the silence of the luxurious resort room. For a moment, his gaze drifted to the blank ceiling above, as if searching for answers. He had hidden himself long enough. The concealment had served its purpose. But now, the only way forward was through the fire.

He needed a plan that would achieve three objectives:

Split Raj and Lucas.

Draw them out into the open.

Make them destroy each other.

The brilliance of the plan was in its simplicity. Give two paranoid, greedy men a reason to suspect each other. Feed them both the same lie—but twist it just enough so they cannot fully trust what the other might do.

Leo began to craft a web of misinformation. He employed burner phones, encrypted messages, and intermediaries, who were unaware that they were mere pawns. Initially, a whisper reached Lucas's trusted lieutenant: the stolen diamonds had reappeared—secured in the old warehouse where everything had begun. Alongside them were two hard drives holding blackmail materials capable of toppling Raj's business empire.

Then, he sent word to Raj. A different angle, the same hook. Leo's last move.

Leo knew both men well enough to anticipate their reactions.

Lucas aimed to safeguard the diamonds and eliminate any compromising files. His priority was to take back control.

Raj, however, couldn't shake the feeling that Lucas had been hiding something from him all along. The thought that his partner might betray him for the loot was enough to stir up that familiar Gambhir paranoia in him.

But there was another layer to it—one not originating from strategy, but from pain instead.

Leo still vividly remembered the night he took Dev's life. It wasn't just about pulling the trigger—what stayed with him was the emptiness that followed. He could never forget what happened to Liza. There was no feeling of triumph, only a deep, painful silence. Even now, the haunting image of Maddy's lifeless eyes remains in his mind, more powerful than any bullet wound ever was.

This was no longer an act of revenge.

This was the moment of reckoning.

Leo understood that Raj and Lucas wouldn't trust each other upon arrival. Each would come with men—armed, alert, yet not aligned. That was the brilliance of it: he didn't need to orchestrate their downfall; they would do it themselves.

He could already hear their voices.

Raj: "You knew about this all along. You think I wouldn't find out?"

Lucas: "Don't be foolish, Raj. This smells like Leo. He's playing us."

Raj: "So you just happened to show up at the same place, same time, for no reason?"

Lucas: "You brought your men. Why would you bring men if you didn't plan on pulling something?"

Raj: "Because I don't trust *you*."

The warehouse would become a crucible—one ultimate test of their greed, hatred, and ego.

Leo didn't have to do the killing himself.

He just needed to light the fuse.

Then, walk away.

He gazed at the laptop he had taken from Maddy's room one last time before shutting it down and packing it into a duffel bag. The final messages had been sent. The trap was set.

Then he made one quick call to Mumbai.

Now, all that was left was for two men to walk into a trap disguised as an opportunity, and for one man, Leo Carlos, to finally reclaim his name.

And once the dust had settled, no kings would remain standing.

Only ghosts.

Chapter 20
The Final Showdown

The docks are eerily silent as night devours the last remnants of daylight. The salty breeze carries whispers of the tide, but beneath it lurks something darker. An unspoken promise of violence. Cranes loom like silent sentinels, while rusted containers cast jagged shadows, and the cold steel of the abandoned shipyard hums with a sense of foreboding.

Lucas is the first to arrive.

His convoy of black SUVs rolls into the deserted yard, headlights piercing through the thick fog like knives. The engines cut out, yet the tension remains. His men move with grim efficiency, patrolling the perimeter and checking every shadow and rooftop. They are loyal, hardened enforcers who have spilt blood for Lucas for years. He steps out last, a thick wool coat hugging his sturdy frame, gold rings catching the light as he adjusts his cuffs. He carries himself like a man who has survived wars–because he has. In the alleys of Anjuna, the ports of Vasco, and the private lounges of Dubai, Lucas has built his empire on brutality and fear. Tonight, he comes not to talk–but to collect.

Minutes later, Raj's convoy arrives, moving more slowly and more quietly.

His approach is precise. Three armoured vehicles, low-beam lights, and bodyguards who form a tight circle the moment he steps out. Raj is dressed in a tailored navy suit, unbuttoned at the top and without a tie. There is a calculated ease about him. Unlike Lucas, Raj has not come from the streets. He has risen through the finance scams, property schemes, and shell companies, laundering blood money until it smells like old wine. He doesn't shout; he negotiates. He bribes, blackmails, and buries problems beneath legal documents. But tonight, his patience is thinning.

On the far wall, a monitor flickers, displaying a loop of grainy security footage, images dredged from the past. At first, it shows crates being shifted, shadows moving in the dim light. Then the moment comes: a suitcase exchanged, Raj's unmistakable frame frozen mid-gesture, accepting it from a figure dressed uncannily like a younger Leo. The clip jitters, repeats, and the image smears just enough to cast doubt but not enough to erase recognition.

The bait is irresistible.

Raj stiffens, his broad shoulders tensing beneath his tailored coat. His eyes narrow, fixed on the incriminating image. The date in the corner is unmistakable. Five-year-old.

Lucas follows his gaze, his expression hardening as he takes in the footage. The sight of Raj caught red-handed, at least to the eye, ignites something raw in him. His teeth grit, and he takes a step forward, voice thick with accusation.

Two kings of the underworld find themselves at a crossroads of betrayal, in a symbolic warehouse that once held their shared sins.

The warehouse, a skeletal relic by the docks, looms over the midnight river like a monument to everything Raj and Lucas have built and destroyed. Its pitted and stained brick walls have borne witness to years of secrets: the hush of illicit dealings, the screams that echo after midnight, the laughter of men who consider themselves untouchable. Now, the warehouse stands silent, save for the distant clang of a buoy and the restless wind slipping through broken windows. Tonight, the past emerges dramatically, demanding attention.

"You bastard," Lucas growls, locking eyes with Raj. "You're the one who set me up that night, aren't you?"

Raj raises an eyebrow, pretending to be confused. "Don't be ridiculous."

Lucas steps closer, the tension between them palpable. "I lost my trusted aide that night."

Raj sneers, his lips curling in contempt. "You're losing your mind. This is clearly your handiwork. What, did you plant this nonsense to get ahead of me again?"

"Lies!" Lucas spits, his hand hovering near his holster; the threat remains unspoken but unmistakable.

The standoff breaks apart, and the atmosphere between them shatters like glass.

The first shot doesn't come from Lucas.

It erupts from the shadows above, a muted rifle crack, swift and precise. One of Lucas's men, stationed near the eastern gate, collapses with a dull thud. No scream. No warning.

Then another. A man from Raj's crew crumples behind the third SUV.

Panic erupts like wildfire. Men shout, guns drawn in every direction, yet there is no target. The shooter remains unseen.

Liza, crouched atop a partly collapsed crane, chambers her next round.

She exhales slowly.

Leo had not only trained her to shoot but also to wait, to breathe, and to strike only when the rhythm of chaos aligned. Tonight, she was silent death. Every bullet was a calculated act of retribution.

Below, chaos boils.

Raj ducks behind a crate, shouting orders. "Find the shooter! Fan out–now!"

Lucas's men hesitate, trying to grasp what is happening and whether Raj's men might be laying an ambush. That little pause costs them.

One of Lucas's lieutenants takes a shot to the throat. Blood sprays across the metal walls as his body convulses before collapsing.

Another shot. Then another. And yet another.

Leo moves along the upper catwalk, his eyes fixed on the carnage below. He doesn't flinch at the gunfire; he has witnessed too much and survived too many nights like this. But this time, it feels different.

This time, he is no longer the hunted.

Liza's aim shifts once more. Her rifle fixes on a man attempting to flank Raj's SUV. She recognises him–Shiva, Lucas's veteran enforcer. Dangerous. Loyal.

A moment later, Shiva collapses, his weapon clattering against the concrete.

Raj's men open fire blindly at the rooftops, their shots full of desperation and aimlessness. One of them, trying to flank from the west, runs straight into a tripwire Leo set hours earlier. This triggers an explosion that tears through the side wall, taking two more.

Screams.

Blood.

Smoke.

Lucas, now bleeding from a cut on his forehead, shouts for his men to retreat. But retreat to where? Every exit is either rigged, blocked, or already compromised. He glances at Raj, who crouches behind a stack of containers.

"You planned this, didn't you?" Lucas yells. "You planned the whole damn thing!"

Raj glares back, teeth bared. "You think I'd walk into this mess and bring my best men if I planned it?"

"Then who?"

Another shot.

Lucas turns just in time to see his driver take a bullet to the chest.

He roars and fires wildly into the air, bullets ricocheting off steel beams.

That's when Leo steps forward.

Not emerging from the shadows but from the smoke.

Gun in hand.

Calm. Composed.

Raj and Lucas stand frozen, disbelief evident on their faces. For a moment, the warehouse hangs in tense, breathless silence. Under the harsh glare of the overhead lights, Leo emerges—his silhouette stark, his expression unreadable, his presence radiating finality. He seems more like a reckoning than a man. All around them, the floor is littered with bodies—their men, shot down. Only the two of them remain standing. It's as if death has arrived, wearing the face of the one man they both tried—and failed—to defeat.

"Looking for something?" Leo's voice is soft—nearly casual, yet it carries a weight that makes both men tense.

Neither responds. Lucas's hand twitches near his holster. Raj clenches his jaw, masking fear with bravado.

Leo steps over a corpse. His gaze holds them both. "You don't start a war unless you're prepared to end it." He lets the silence hang. "You both started this long ago. Tonight, I'm just tying up loose ends."

Raj finds his voice, though it is strained with anger. "You think you can walk in here—play judge, jury, executioner? You're nothing, Leo. You never were."

Lucas reaches for his weapon, but Leo reacts more quickly. A single shot to the chest causes the crime lord to stumble backwards, blood blooming like a crimson flower on his shirt.

Another shot.

Lucas drops dead flat on the floor.

Raj lets out a terrified scream, stumbling backwards as his shoes scrape against the damp concrete of the dock. His arms flail behind him, searching for something–anything–to anchor him. But there is nothing. Only the chilling wind, the lapping water, and the unmistakable look of death in Leo's eyes.

"Please, Leo wait," Raj gasps, his voice cracking. His face, once full of arrogant charm, twists in panic. "We can talk about this."

Leo looms over him, shadows cloaking his figure like armour. His voice is calm and steady–more terrifying than a scream. "You framed me. You threatened my family. You killed Maddy."

Raj shakes his head violently, his eyes wide. "No! No, it wasn't me. It was Lucas! He's the one who gave the order. I tried to stop it!"

Leo's jaw tightens. "Don't lie to me. Maybe Lucas pulled the trigger, but you lit the match."

Raj's mouth opens and closes, searching for words. Then, like a drowning man grasping for a rope, he babbles, his desperation evident. "He was out of control, Leo. You know how he is. You were his right hand once. You saw what he did to people who got in his way."

Leo says nothing, yet his silence was more potent than rage. The gun in his hand remains steady.

Raj's eyes dart to the side, catching a glint of metal, his own pistol, just out of reach.

"I didn't want Maddy dead," Raj pleads, his voice trembling so hard it nearly breaks. His eyes shine with tears, the bravado stripped away, leaving only raw panic. "She was... collateral. I swear to you, Leo. I didn't want it to go that far."

He gulps, words tumbling out in a frantic rush. "I told Lucas it would attract heat, that it would bring everything crashing down, but he wouldn't listen. He said it was the only way to get to you."

Raj's chest heaves as he struggles to catch his breath. His hands tremble at his sides, fingers twitching as if resisting the urge to claw the air for mercy. "Please, Leo," he chokes out, voice cracking. "I'm not your enemy. Lucas... he dragged me in. I tried to stop it. I swear on my life, I tried. I never wanted her dead."

A shiver runs through him, and he quickly continues, desperation flooding his words. "And Liza... Dev made a grave mistake. He didn't know what he was doing. I'm sorry—really sorry. Please spare me."

He takes a step closer, eyes wide with frantic hope. "We can fix this. I'll help you. Just... don't pull that trigger."

Raj, ever the survivor, reaches for his gun—yet Leo is already there. He presses the barrel against Raj's forehead.

"For my sister," Leo murmurs. And he looks up.

A single shot into Raj's head.

As the final body hits the ground, silence descends on the night. The only sounds are the distant crashing of waves against the cliffs and the gentle rustling of palm trees swaying in the night breeze. The scent of gunpowder still lingers in the air, mingling with the salt and blood that soak the earth. The battlefield has become a graveyard—Raj Gambhir and Lucas Dada lie motionless, their reign of terror finally at an end.

Liza exhales quietly, carefully lowering herself from her perch atop the crumbling rooftop. Below, the city's neon lights shimmer softly, but her focus remains on the moment—the distant echo of gunfire and the adrenaline still coursing through her veins. The sniper rifle slung across her back, the very tool that helped secure their victory tonight, feels comfortable and familiar in her hands. She moves with quiet confidence, having long since relinquished any illusions of innocence. Her face, once open and expressive, now bears a calm, unreadable mask—focused and resolute. There's no fear in her heart, no regret—just a cool, precise sense of satisfaction from justice served and debts paid.

The journey to this point had been a remarkable story, full of loss, change, and a fierce resolve to survive. After that unforgettable night—when the old world was left behind and only questions about the future remained—Liza and her mother, Elena, disappeared into the chaos. They abandoned their homes, memories of hunger and fear, and the spirits of men who had underestimated them. Their new destination was Mumbai, a city as vast and unyielding as the ocean itself, where Leo had already begun to make his mark in the shadows.

Mumbai felt like an entirely new world compared to the cosy coastal village of their childhood. The city thumped with life, its bustling streets brimming with energy from millions of people–some chasing their dreams, others fleeing from their nightmares. Towering skylines glistened under the sun, while the sea breeze carried whispers of endless possibilities. For every weary soul, the city still held the promise of reinvention, of a tomorrow brighter than yesterday. For Liza, being in the city was both overwhelming and exciting. It offered her the freedom to be herself and start anew, but it also demanded strength, cleverness, and a great deal of adaptability. She observed her brother navigate this busy world with a mix of pride and worry. Leo had changed considerably–he was tougher, smarter, but still carried that same strong loyalty that once made him her hero.

Elena, for her part, opened a bakery on the outskirts of the city, her hands as skilled as ever and her spirit quietly resilient. She and Liza shared an apartment above the shop, with thin walls and an air thick with the scent of yeast and cardamom. At night, they sat together, speaking little and each lost in her own thoughts. Elena seldom spoke of the past, but Liza could see the toll it had taken; her eyes were lined with worry and her sighs were heavy with weight. Yet, there was a sense of safety in their new life, a fragile peace that neither fully trusted.

Leo was the first to suggest that Liza join him. He watched how quickly she adapted to the city, carefully observing and listening, absorbing its rhythms and secrets. He recognised in her the same drive that had propelled him—the urge to never feel powerless again. At first, Liza hesitated. She remembered the violence, the betrayals, and the consequences of the world Leo now lived in. But she also recalled their past helplessness: the nights waiting for a father who never returned, and the days surviving on hope and scraps. She resolved that she would no longer be a victim.

Training started quietly in the early hours before dawn. Leo patiently shared his knowledge of marksmanship, combat skills, and how to navigate the city's intricate streets silently. He introduced her to his trusted network of contacts, informants, and allies who exchanged information and favours. Liza picked it up swiftly; her mind was sharp and her instincts even sharper. She learned to read others' intentions, anticipate potential dangers, and conceal her feelings behind a composed exterior. She was no longer the barefoot girl who laughed at hardship. She had become a skilled fighter, always prepared for whatever lay ahead.

Over the years, Liza's role within Leo's organisation grew considerably. She became his trusted partner, adept at gathering intelligence, closing deals, and, when needed, enforcing rules with a detached efficiency that even her brother found admirable. She operated from the shadows, her name spoken with a mix of fear and respect. Those who underestimated her soon realised they should not make the same mistake.

Liza went beyond mere enforcement; she brought a fresh, invigorating perspective to Leo's business. She emphasised the importance of strategic planning and understanding predator-prey behaviour, which added depth to their approach. She encouraged Leo to explore new opportunities and invest in reputable ventures, opening up many possibilities. Together, they built an extensive network that covered the city, from modest neighbourhoods to luxurious high-rises. Liza became skilled at carefully managing power, cleverly turning competitors against each other and staying one step ahead of any threats, even before they materialised.

Despite her growing reputation, Liza always focused on what truly mattered. She was intensely protective of Elena, constantly looking out for her mother and shielding her from anything unpleasant. Every week, she visited the bakery with gifts and stories, doing her best to keep things feeling normal. Sometimes, she would pause and imagine what her father might think if he could see her now – the strong young woman she had become, who had not only survived difficult times but also thrived despite them.

There were nights when it felt like the weight of everything was simply too much for her to bear. The violence, the secrets, and the realisation that every choice had its cost- all of it could be overwhelming. However, over time, Liza had discovered a way to live alongside the darkness. She understood that in their world, justice wasn't always about courtrooms or officials in uniform; it was often whispered in hushed tones or delivered with silent bullets, finding its resolution in the quiet moments when old debts were finally settled.

Through it all, Leo and Liza remained committed partners. United by blood, shared history, and the unspoken vow that they would never allow the world to take from them what they refused to relinquish. They trusted each other completely, their bond forged through hardship and strengthened by the fires of ambition.

Liza's journey reached a crucial point when she confidently stood on the rooftop, rifle in hand, her eyes calm and resolute. No longer simply fleeing her past, she was now actively shaping her future, making deliberate moves with purpose. The city beneath her belonged to those brave enough to seize it, and Liza Carlos was finally prepared to claim her rightful share. It was not vengeance that drove her, but survival and the realisation that, at last, she was the one writing her story.

She and Leo exchange a glance. No words are necessary. Everything that needs to be said is communicated through blood and bullets. The job is finished. Their enemies are dead. However, they both understand what lies ahead. There is no celebration in their world–only survival.

Leo wipes a streak of blood from his face, surveying the carnage around him. For a moment, he feels nothing. Not relief, not triumph–just a quiet emptiness. Perhaps this is what closure feels like. Or maybe it is simply another chapter ending, another war fought with no real victory. He turns to Liza and gently presses her hand. "You know what to do."

She nods once. In the distance, faint sirens begin to wail. They have only minutes before the police arrive. It doesn't matter. They are ghosts–always have been. And ghosts never stay longer than they need to.

When Detective Aamir arrived, he found the scene already quiet, but the atmosphere was heavy. Walking onto the bloodstained docks with his hands in his pockets, he took in the sight with a faint smirk. Having seen many crime scenes before, he knew this one was different. It wasn't just a gang fight–it felt more like a cleansing.

The bodies of Raj and Lucas lay inches apart, their hands still clutching their guns in death. Around them, their most trusted men lay scattered, executed with deadly precision. It was almost poetic–two kings of the underworld brought down by their own folly.

Aamir crouched beside Raj's corpse, studying the wound. "Clean shot," he muttered. "No hesitation." He looked around at the others. Sniper fire. Close-range kills. It had been a coordinated attack, executed flawlessly.

He stood and let out a soft chuckle. "Well played, Leo. Well played."

The official story would be easy to spin. A fallout between Raj and Lucas: greed, betrayal, a typical underworld feud that spiralled into mutual destruction. It wasn't even a lie, just a version of the truth dressed up as fiction. Aamir had no intention of digging deeper.

He looked out towards the horizon, where the ocean appeared to stretch endlessly into the night. Out there somewhere, Leo had vanished again, just like five years ago, just like before.

For years, the name Leo drifted through the criminal underworld like smoke–light, elusive, and always just out of reach. Tales of his ascent, fall, and mysterious disappearance have become akin to folklore among thieves, hitmen, and smugglers. Some believed he was dead; others claimed they had seen him on distant shores, hiding behind false names and new faces. But the truth remained a mystery.

Aamir stood silently in the alley, the scent of ash and blood still hanging in the air. He offered a small smile as he turned away from the scene, his coat fluttering faintly in the breeze. The dead could keep their secrets for now. His focus had shifted. His path was now clear.

A new task has emerged that requires more than just investigative skills. The goal is clear: to find Leo Carlos. However, it's not enough merely to locate him; Aamir must also understand him, grasp his complexity and attempt to anticipate his actions, as he no longer adheres to society's usual norms. Aamir acknowledges that this will be a tough challenge. Leo isn't just a fugitive; he's like a myth, cloaked in survival and mystery, which makes him even more difficult to comprehend.

But Aamir relished the challenge. For him, this wasn't just another case; it was a quest that would test every ounce of his patience, instinct, and resolve. The hunt had begun, and somewhere out there, Leo was already on the move.

Chapter 21
Echoes on the Shore

The salt-laden wind whipped around the deserted docks, carrying the faint smell of gunpowder and the unmistakable stillness that follows a storm. Detective Aamir examined the scene: Raj Gambhir and Lucas Dada lay dead, their reign over Goa's underworld ended in a final, bloody clash. Around them, their enforcers stood silently, witnesses to a power shift orchestrated by the ghost of their past.

Aamir recognised the precision of the kills and the calculated elimination of threats. It was the work of someone who understood the game intimately, driven by a deep-seated need for justice. He pieced together the narrative: Leo Carlos had returned, not as a fugitive, but as a reckoning. The stolen fortune had been the catalyst, but the fuel was vengeance for his sister, Liza.

Leo had spent years in the shadows, patiently awaiting the right moment to reclaim what was his. He was once a promising fighter, driven by dreams beyond the bloody streets of Goa. However, life took a different turn. Lucas Dada, the crime boss who used to be his mentor, held Leo captive with the heavy chains of the underworld. Raj Gambhir, the ruthless businessman who used crime to get what he wanted, ensured Leo had no escape.

Liza had been the only reason Leo ever wanted more. She had been his anchor, a reminder that something pure still existed in his life. But when violence spilt into his home, and Raj Gambhir made her collateral in his relentless quest for power, Leo's world went up in flames. He fled then, a broken man, carrying only the scars of betrayal and the burden of his sister's pain.

But exile had not softened him. If anything, it had sharpened him into something more dangerous. He had travelled, learned, and adapted. He had made powerful allies, gathered intelligence, and waited for the right moment to strike. He hadn't returned to Goa as a desperate man seeking redemption–he had returned as an executioner.

The docks became the final battleground. There was never any intention of reaching an agreement. Leo's return was carefully orchestrated, knowing that the only way to dismantle the criminal empire was to eliminate its leader. Through strategic deception, he sowed discord, dividing allies and causing chaos within their ranks. Raj and Lucas walked straight into his trap, unaware that Leo had plotted their downfall from the shadows.

Liza had also been there. No longer the frightened girl he once vowed to protect, she had become a warrior in her own right. She trained, learned how to fight, and, more importantly, learned to survive in a world that had tried to break her. It was she who fired the shot that ended Raj's life, her hands steady and her resolve unshaken. Leo had personally dealt with Lucas, a final act of severing the ties that had once bound him.

That night, the streets of Goa underwent a profound change. The old power structures fell apart, and a new reality started to emerge.

But Leo and Liza had already disappeared into the night like spirits, leaving nothing but a legend behind. The wind carried away the echoes of the past, yet the message endured: power built on blood and treachery would always crumble. The weak could rise, the hunted could become the hunters, and sometimes, justice was not about law but about balance. In the end, the streets of Goa would never forget the night Leo returned.

Aamir grasped the unspoken truth: the cycle of violence, born in the streets of Panaji, had come full circle. The powerful had preyed on the weak, and the weak, when pushed to their limits, had risen to challenge their oppressors.

Leo Carlos's story did not begin on that fateful night at the docks. Instead, it started in the quiet, neglected alleyways where a young boy struggled to survive, learning early that the world can be harsh on those who are vulnerable. His fists became his first teachers, and his resilience was all he had to defend himself. When Lucas kindly took him under his wing, Leo thought he saw a way to a brighter future. But sadly, he was actually drawn further into the darkness he desperately wished to escape.

Years in exile had hardened him, but they also brought clarity. He had returned not to reclaim what was lost, but to ensure that the past could never hurt him or Liza again. He had become more than a fighter—he had become a hunter, his every move precise, his revenge carefully planned.

The plan had been set in motion long before the final confrontation. Leo had successfully infiltrated Raj's inner circle, planting seeds of distrust and doubt. Lucas posed his greatest challenge. Once he had been like a father figure, but Leo recognised that such feelings no longer mattered in the world they inhabited. When the moment arrived, he showed no hesitation.

The gentle whisper of the Goan breeze reveals a simple truth: the streets hold memories. They serve as living witnesses to both hardship and hope. While power gained through exploitation and fear can seem daunting, the human spirit guided by family ties and a desire for justice can emerge from the shadows and forge a new future. The cost of unjust power will inevitably be paid, even if it takes years for the echoes of past injustices to fade on the shore.

The sun dips low on the horizon, casting a beautiful golden glow over the peaceful waters as the cruise liner gently sails through the Arabian Sea towards the west. Leo stands on the upper deck, happy to feel the warm breeze on his face while he softly wraps his arm around Elena's shoulder. Nearby, Liza giggles happily as she chases seagulls fluttering close to the railings. For the first time in months, perhaps even years, they seem like a truly happy family.

Yet, behind their gentle smiles and shared moments of happiness, the unmistakable burden of what they left behind in Goa still lingers–its chaos, corruption, and the chilling presence of the law. Leo can still feel its echo within him; the tension in his shoulders stubbornly refuses relief. They have indeed managed to escape—but it isn't true freedom, at least not yet.

Elena rests her head on Leo's shoulder, her eyes scanning the boundless blue. "It feels like a dream," she whispers, her voice tinged with disbelief and fatigue.

Leo tightens his grip on her shoulder and kisses her forehead. "We made it, Mum. We're here. We've got Liza, we've got each other. That's all that matters." She turns to face him, her eyes searching his. "But for how long?" she asks.

He doesn't lie. "As long as we can keep moving. As long as we stay sharp."

Leo pauses, lost in a fleeting memory of Maddy. A single tear slides down his cheek. He longs for her presence, the warmth of her voice, the comfort of her touch. In that quiet moment, he wishes more than anything that she could be there beside him once again.

Below them, the cruise lights shimmer like scattered jewels on the midnight water, while soft jazz drifts through the warm night air, blending with bursts of laughter and the delicate clinking of glasses from the lively restaurant. It all feels almost surreal—the polished glow of the wooden decks, the salty whisper of the sea breeze against his skin, and the infinite stars glittering overhead like silent witnesses.

Elena gently pulls Leo and Liza into a warm, trembling embrace. The siblings snuggle close, their small arms wrapping around her, hiding their faces in her comforting warmth. For a fleeting moment, it feels as if time stands still, a tender moment built on love, shared scars, and a strong desire to keep moving forward against all odds.

When Leo's eyes open again, an intense wave of protectiveness floods him. Beneath it all, one name echoes in his mind, an icy shard lodged in his thoughts: Detective Aamir.

But that is a story for another time. For now, as the vast ocean stretches endlessly before them and the stars glitter softly overhead, Leo allows himself the rare luxury of hope, something he hasn't felt in years. The waves whisper quiet promises, the breeze carries a hush of calm and serenity, and for the first time in a long while, he lets himself breathe.

He knows that the future still holds shadows. One day, the past will come crashing back, demanding its reckoning in blood and truth. But tonight, in this delicate, stolen moment of peace, he has found something worth fighting for. And when that reckoning arrives, he will defend it with everything he has—even if it costs him his life.

THE END